D1175852

Everyday Strategic Preparedness

Everyday Strategic Preparedness

The Role of Practical Wisdom in Organizations

Matt Statler
Associate Director, International Center for Enterprise Preparedness (InterCEP), New York University (NYU), USA; Former Director of Research, Imagination Lab Foundation

Johan Roos
Bo Rydin and SCA Professor of Strategy and Dean of MBA Programs, Stockholm School of Economics (SSE); Sweden Former Director, Imagination Lab Foundation

First published 2007 by
PALGRAVE MACMILLAN
Houndmills, Basingstoke, Hampshire RG21 6XS and
175 Fifth Avenue, New York, N.Y. 10010
Companies and representatives throughout the world

PALGRAVE MACMILLAN is the global academic imprint of the Palgrave Macmillan division of St. Martin's Press, LLC and of Palgrave Macmillan Ltd. Macmillan® is a registered trademark in the United States, United Kingdom and other countries. Palgrave is a registered trademark in the European Union and other countries.

ISBN-13: 978–0–230–51563–5   hardback
ISBN-10: 0–230–51563–0   hardback

This book is printed on paper suitable for recycling and made from fully managed and sustained forest sources. Logging, pulping and manufacturing processes are expected to conform to the environmental regulations of the country of origin.

A catalogue record for this book is available from the British Library.

Library of Congress Cataloging-in-Publication Data
Statler, Matt.
    Everyday strategic preparedness: the role of practical wisdom in organization / Matt Statler, Johan Roos.
        p. cm.
    Includes bibliographical references and index.
    ISBN-13: 978–0–230–51563–5 (cloth)
    ISBN-10: 0–230–51563–0 (cloth)
        1. Strategic planning. 2. Organizational effectiveness. 3. Executive ability. I. Roos, Johan. II. Title.

HD30.28.S695 2007
658.4'012–dc22   2006051748

        1.

10   9   8   7   6   5   4   3   2   1
16   15   14   13   12   11   10   09   08   07

Printed and bound in Great Britain by
Antony Rowe Ltd, Chippenham and Eastbourne

To our beloved and supportive wives
Roxanna and Madeleine

Contents

List of Figures

Note: Figures developed with the support of Ryan Hagen.

xi

Acknowledgements

We acknowledge the productive research environment at the Imagination Lab Foundation, especially including our interactions with the following colleagues and collaborators: Peter Buergi, Cliff Dennett, Jennie Gertun-Olsson, Francois Grey, Greg Holliday, Claus Jacobs, Wendelin Kuepers, Hugo Letiche, Marc-Olivier Linder, Marjorie Lyles, Mark Marotto, Joyce Miller, David Oliver, Karin Oppegaard, Dave Owens, Jim Prouty, Richard Randell, Jim Rowe, Roger Said, Susan Schneider, Carla Svehlik, and Bart Victor.

0.0
Background and Motivation

This book presents an account of a series of explorations that took place between 2002 and 2005 at the Imagination Lab Foundation, an independent and nonprofit research organization based in Switzerland.

During this time, we have been in constant contact with two adjacent but distinct groups: (i) people who work as organizational leaders, managers and strategists, and (ii) people who work as academic researchers and teachers in the discipline of management and organizational studies. We have engaged alongside the practitioners as collaborators and participant-observers, contributing to and gathering data about organizational strategy practices. In turn, we have participated in the community of researchers, presenting our findings and reflections in Europe and the US in the form of journal submissions, conference papers and informal conversations with academic colleagues.

In these dialogues, we have focused our attention on the practice of strategic management, on what people actually do in organizations when they are 'practicing strategy'. More specifically, we have focused on serious play[1] as a

---

[1] The concept of 'serious play' as used in this book has been developed and elaborated in the following publications: Roos, J., and B. Victor,

1

particular mode of practice that can improve, extend, cast new light on, or qualitatively enhance strategic management as it is practiced in organizations.[2]

In this regard, we have found ourselves consistently wondering about the unique human capabilities that can be developed when people engage in playful and multi-modal forms of practice. Different research streams in the social sciences have pursued this question in considerable depth.[3] For example, in the constructivist tradition of learning and educational research, play has been shown to involve the development of basic cognitive functions such as assimilation and accommodation. Among psychologists and sociologists, play has also been considered

---

'Towards a Model of Strategy Making as Serious Play' (1999), *European Management Journal* 17(4): 348–55; Roos, J., Victor, B., and Statler, M. 'Playing Seriously with Strategy' (2004), *Long Range Planning*, December 37/6, pp. 549–68; Jacobs, C. and Statler, M. 'Strategy Creation as Serious Play' (2005), Floyd, S., Roos, J., Jacobs, C., and Kellermans, F. (eds.), in *Innovating Strategy Process*, Blackwell; Jacobs, C. and Statler, M. (2006) 'Toward a Technology of Foolishness – Developing Scenarios through Serious Play' *International Studies of Management and Organisation*, 36(3): 77–92; Statler, M., 'Practical Wisdom and Serious Play: Reflections on Management Understanding' (2005), in Schrat, H. (ed.), *Sophisticated Survival Techniques/Strategies in Art and Economy*, Berlin: Kulturverlag Kadmos.

[2] Johan Roos has subsequently extended this concept to also include ways to boost intuition and improvisation, through cultivating a state of spontaneity, by using non-scripted dramatic methods. See Roos, J. (2006) *Thinking from Within: A Hands-On Strategy Practice*, Basingstoke: Palgrave Macmillan. For a review and definition of spontaneity as a state of mind, see Roos, J., and M. Roos, 'On Spontaneity' (2006), Working Paper 72, Imagination Lab Foundation, Switzerland (www.imagilab.org).

[3] Our comprehensive review of psychological, sociological, anthropological and philosophical theories of play is presented in Statler, M., Roos, J., and Victor, B. (2002) ' "Ain't Misbehavin" ': Taking Play Seriously in Organizations.' Working Paper 17, Imagination Lab Foundation, Switzerland (www.imagilab.org).

as the activity through which the capacity to make meaning in social contexts is developed. On the most primary level, psychoanalysts have argued that 'play' names the healthy exploration of object-relations and self-identification processes.

In view of these various accounts of the importance of play for human development, we began to wonder more precisely: to what extent have these various cognitive, social and emotional outcomes of play been considered as an integrated phenomenon, as an ability or capacity which might be cultivated more deliberately, especially in organizational contexts?

In response to this question, it was the work of social theorists and philosophers such as Bourdieu, de Certeau and Gadamer that pointed us directly toward the notion that these various intelligent and yet embodied capabilities identified by different scholarly traditions as outcomes of 'serious play' might be considered as an integrated phenomenon, namely, as practical wisdom.[4]

As far back as Aristotle, practical wisdom has been identified as the virtue of the leader or statesman who can, even in the face of extreme uncertainty and ambiguity, make decisions and take actions that are effective as well as ethical. Intrigued by this suggestion and compelled by the ancient tradition supporting it, we started to re-focus our strategy research questions beyond the practice of serious play, and toward practical wisdom and its relevance for organizations. What would practical wisdom look

---

[4] Cf. Bourdieu, P. (1998) *Practical Reason*, Stanford: Stanford University Press; Gadamer, H.G. (2002 [1960]) *Truth and Method*, New York: Continuum; de Certeau, M. (1984) *The Practice of Everyday Life*, Berkeley: University of California Press. See also chapter 13 in Roos, J. (2006) *Thinking from Within: A Hands-On Strategy Practice*, Basingstoke: Palgrave Macmillan.

like in the empirical context of strategy practice? What might the impacts of practical wisdom be for contemporary organizations?

At around the time that these questions were taking shape in our conversations, we established contact with a group of people at New York University (NYU) in the newly-created Center for Catastrophe Preparedness and Response (CCPR).[5] Over eight months of regular conversations and interactions with them in 2003 and early 2004, we became aware that a field of strategy practices is currently emerging around a need for preparedness that appears endemic to our complex and uncertain contemporary world.

The broad horizons of this field are referred to using terms such as: catastrophe preparedness, disaster preparedness, business continuity, risk management, and so on. To be sure, this field has grown to prominence previously in different forms and on a smaller scale, most notably in the aftermath of Bhopal, and in response to a series of ecological disasters.[6] But following the events of September 11, 2001, this field has grown and changed dramatically. CCPR was itself created with a direct congressional allocation in the aftermath of September 11, and its mission was to serve as a resource center for preparedness-related research and education. As such, it provided us with an initial (and particularly well-placed) lens through which to examine the challenge of preparedness as it confronts contemporary organizations.

---

[5] In January 2006, after this manuscript was completed, Matt Statler became the Associate Director of the International Center for Enterprise Preparedness (InterCEP), a program developed by CCPR with a specific focus on preparedness in the private sector.

[6] In this regard, the work of Ian Mitroff has been most influential on the field of crisis management: cf. his watershed *Corporate Tragedies, Product Tampering, Sabotage, and Other Catastrophes*, with Ralph Kilmann, New York: Praeger 1984.

Thus we found ourselves motivated by the strategic 'need for preparedness', as well as fascinated by the large-scale investment and intense human energy being devoted to it all around us in the 'preparedness field'. So we started to consider the field in which the need for preparedness is dealt with as the empirical context for our reflections on practical wisdom. The question that gave rise to this book is: *how can organizations facing a strategic need for preparedness benefit from practical wisdom?*

We should preface our response to this question by emphasizing the fact that we found ourselves investigating practical wisdom in the field of preparedness by following our primary interest in those seriously playful practices through which people develop and exercise their minds, engage with their social milieu, and undergo intense affective dynamics. We should also note that our research focused on serious play was itself motivated by a pragmatic interest in generating new knowledge about strategic practices in such way as to enable those practices to improve.

Thus at the level of our own assumptions, we should confess a series of biases: (i) to focus on aesthetically- and experientially-rich aspects of organizational practice, (ii) to consider the ways in which those practices may be developed or deliberately cultivated, and (iii) to judge the value of those practices by the extent to which they appear to contribute to the strategic need for preparedness in organizations.

In this light, while we acknowledge the importance of formal, mathematical risk analysis and decision modeling as methods of enhancing organizational preparedness, we are biased to be interested instead in those aspects of intelligent human action that may not easily be represented in a metric or an algorithm. Put differently, we are more inclined to focus on the human social practice of using algorithms than on the algorithms themselves. As researchers in the field of strategic management, we have been trained to accept as an article of faith the notion that even when advanced mathematical models and statistical analyses back up strategic plans they nevertheless require effective implementation in practice.[7] Through our collaborations with strategists, leaders and managers, we have also come to accept the ontological claim (put forth by complex adaptive systems theorists as well as stock analysts) that even when the best-laid strategic plans are implemented with expert skill and coordination, an organization's effectiveness can still be radically disrupted by unforeseen events (whether in the extreme case of 9/11 or in the generic, butterfly effect of a market fluctuation).

So as we seek in this book to explore how different forms or modes of practice might contribute to (or detract from) an organization's preparedness, our basic hunch is that, in addition to analytically-grounded strategic plans and top-down change processes, *organizations require a measure of 'practical wisdom' in order to be strategically prepared for unexpected change.*

As we begin to explore this hunch in the following pages, we also feel an obligation to acknowledge certain constraints that arise from the format we have selected for our explorations. A self-referential gesture: you are currently reading a series of reflections presented in a book. If we were critically to evaluate this format as a kind of seriously playful, embodied experiential learning, it would fall considerably short of the ideal. And yet since practical wisdom may also be developed through narrative genres, we simply need to be explicit about what form of

---

[7] Recall, for example, the familiar adage about strategy being 10% inspiration and 90% implementation.

practice this book is, while remaining critical with respect to the inter-subjective and material conditions that sustain it.

In this sense, we hope to explore a relatively wide range of concepts and scholarly traditions while following a single thread of argument. Guided by our own academic formations (in the fields of philosophy and strategic management, respectively), we situate our reflections in the context of current discourses in the field of strategic management and organizational studies. More broadly, we reflect on current events, including socio-political and cultural phenomena, while drawing on a series of philosophical concepts. Finally, we illustrate these reflections by weaving in illustrative data drawn both from the public domain as well as from our own empirical research involving strategists and organizational leaders.

We acknowledge that by accepting input from this range of sources, we necessarily sacrifice some degree of discipline or rigor. Indeed, as the broad organizational and societal implications of 'the need for preparedness' become manifest, we risk losing sight of the forest among all the trees.

As a way to overcome this limitation, we call here at the outset for scholarly discussion and debate about whether the concepts of practical wisdom and preparedness as we present them have been properly understood. We anticipate that additional research will be required properly to describe the significance of these concepts in relation to other philosophical and organizational concepts.

While we hope that such debate might unfold in the future, for now our practice remains that of a co-authored monograph, not a dialogue or panel discussion with interlocutors. Working within these constraints, we will acknowledge key points of contention by citing relevant sources in footnotes in the hope that further scholarship and discussion will draw from (and add to) our considerations.

We will additionally strive to adopt a rhetoric that speaks simultaneously to researchers in the academic discipline of strategic management studies, and to reflective managers and organizational leaders. Our hope is that this book might bring these two groups into more direct dialogue with each other,[8] while providing them both with an indication of how practical wisdom can contribute to the organizational need for preparedness.

We also present these reflections with the pragmatic hope that they will help make more rigorous theory development and empirical data gathering possible, and by extension, help develop practical wisdom in the field of strategic management. In this sense, the purpose of this book is *to identify the role of practical wisdom in organizations, with a specific focus on an emerging field of management practice (that is, preparedness) that has not yet been well-documented by strategy researchers.*

The overall flow of the argument that we develop to achieve that purpose is as follows:

- In a world characterized by increased complexity and uncertainty, preparedness becomes the most important strategic challenge for organizations.
- As the need for preparedness stretches the limits of what is thinkable and possible for organizations, the importance of ethics becomes increasingly clear.
- The concept of practical wisdom provides a framework that can guide strategists as they balance ethical demands with demands for practical effectiveness.

---

[8] The relative paucity of dialogue between these two groups was, for example, bemoaned by several of the distinguished panelists in the 2004 symposium session entitled 'Does Organizational Theory Really Matter?' sponsored by the Organizational and Management Theory Division at the Academy of Management Annual Meeting.

- Practical wisdom can be developed through playful activities such as storytelling, reflective dialogue and aesthetic experience.
- By cultivating practical wisdom, people in organizations can develop the everyday strategic preparedness needed to deal with a complex and uncertain world.

1.0

Strategy and Unexpected Change

In a world characterized by increased complexity and uncertainty, organizations today struggle to be strategically prepared for unexpected change. Of course, the strategist's job has traditionally involved an attempt to anticipate changes in the environment and to develop capabilities that will allow the organization to continue to thrive under new and different circumstances. But what if change cannot be anticipated with any degree of certainty? And what if change is so complex that its effects and implications can never be fully understood, much less anticipated? What, if anything, can organizations do to become more strategically prepared for unexpected change?

Our overall response to these difficult questions is that people in organizations become more strategically prepared for the unexpected when they cultivate *practical wisdom*. But what is practical wisdom? How exactly does practical wisdom enable people in organizations to deal with the strategic challenge of preparedness? If practical wisdom does enable people to deal with the strategic challenge of preparedness, then how can it be cultivated?

In the following pages, we will attempt to develop answers to each of these questions, and we will explore the implications of our answers for strategic management theory and practice. At this point, however, we begin by examining the strategic challenge of preparedness more closely, tracing its evolution through a shift in the ontology of strategic management, and defining it in terms of a practical problem that emerges when the limits of thought and action are surpassed by an unexpected event.

2.0
An Ontological Shift

Various scholars have attempted to write *the* definitive history of modern strategic management. *Strategy Safari: A Guided Tour through the Wilds of Strategic Management* (Mintzberg et al., 1998) may be the most widely read such attempt – but there are many others.[9] The narrative that these histories offer has become quite familiar to researchers as well as practitioners: over the course of several decades, what we call 'strategy' has evolved from a business plan that originates in the mind of a long-term visionary leader; to become a process of market analysis undertaken by expert number-crunchers; and, finally, to appear as the adaptive process through which an organizational system makes sense of itself and its environment.

Our endeavor here is not simply to repeat this narrative, nor to supplant it with a new, alternative story. Instead, we

---

[9] These others include both textbooks and journal publications. See Johnson, G. (2004) *Exploring Corporate Strategy Text and Cases*, 7th Edition, London: FT Prentice Hall; Whittington, R. (1993), *What Is Strategy and Does It Matter?* London: Routledge; R.E. Hoskisson et al. (1999) 'Swings of a Pendulum', *Journal of Management* (25) 417–56; Farjoun, M. (2002) 'Towards an Organic Perspective on Strategy' *Strategic Management Journal*, 23(7): 561–94.

wish to emphasize that the field of strategic management has experienced, and continues to experience, a shift in its fundamental ontology. With the term 'ontology', we refer to the basic assumptions about what a strategy *is*, how its constituent parts *relate* to each other, and finally, how these parts undergo *change*. It may not be common for strategists, typically so concerned with ensuring competitive advantage and bottom-line growth, to reflect at any length on such assumptions. And yet we suggest that any shift at the level of these assumptions has profound implications for how organizations frame and respond to the strategic challenge of preparedness.

2.1   Static ontology

As is well known, modern strategic management took shape within the paradigm of scientific management (cf. Taylor, 1911). At an ontological level, this paradigm assumes that fundamentally static laws govern human social systems such as organizations. Thus just as change in the natural environment occurs in accordance with unchanging natural laws, when an organization undergoes change, it does so in accordance with immutable principles of change. And because such laws and principles are not always immediately manifest to the human observer, 'scientific' management addresses the task of discovering, testing, and applying them to organizational systems.

In concrete terms, the specific challenge addressed by strategists working in this paradigm traditionally involves the creation of scientifically-grounded, analytic models that enable the effective management of diversified enterprises (cf. Ansoff, 1965; Hofer and Schendel, 1978; Porter, 1980). To pick up one such model, it may be assumed (a) that the business environment *is* or *consists of* five forces (that is, rivalry, supplier power, buyer power, barriers to entry, and threat of substitutes), (b) that the appropriate competitive strategy can be determined based on an accurate assessment of *the relationship between these various forces*, and (c) that in order to respond strategically to change in the environment, strategists must not develop an entirely new model, but instead *re-apply the model* to determine the appropriate strategy. Or to pick up another, more foundational model of strategic and economic theory, it may be assumed (a) that a market *is* or *consists of* a group of individuals acting in such a way as to maximize their self-interest, (b) that the appropriate price of a good or service can be determined based on an accurate assessment of *the relationship between available supply and demand* for it, and (c) that responding to change in the supply or demand requires only a *re-calculation of the relationship* to determine the appropriate price again.

Our presentation of these two models here provides little more than a caricature – and yet, this caricature can illustrate our point about ontological assumptions. Within this first paradigm, which we refer to as a static ontology, strategists are encouraged to pursue knowledge about the environment and the organization, to make decisions and formulate strategies based on this knowledge, and to implement structures and processes that serve effectively to produce competitive advantage, and, in turn, successful growth (or an alternative performance criterion). In essence, the role of the strategist involves intentionally and efficiently seeking to control the organization's future performance by whatever means appear most effective. The notion that effective strategic control is possible at all depends on the assumption that change occurs in accordance with static principles that can be known scientifically. And in those unfortunate (if inevitable) cases where events or circumstances arise that disrupt the effectiveness of strategy as such, the basic ontological assumptions need not be called into question because fault can always be attributed to a lack of sufficient knowledge, to inadequate decision-making mechanisms, or (as is most common) to a lack of effective implementation.

Our point here is that when strategists operate within this static ontology, then the term 'preparedness' refers to a state of affairs that can be definitively and objectively identified, that is, an outcome variable that can be controlled for with greater or lesser efficiency and effectiveness. The claim, uttered by a strategist or an organizational leader, that 'we are prepared!' is in this light more than just a manner of speaking, and more than just a boast. It represents an ontological claim about what the organization is, what the landscape is, and how the two stand in relation to each other. Within this static ontology, the 'strategic challenge of preparedness' calls for the development of knowledge by which all future possible events may be anticipated, as well as for the design and development of capabilities to handle all the possible consequences of these events adequately to ensure the continued advantage and growth of the organization.

But as strategists confront the difficulty, if not the impossibility, of developing such knowledge and such capabilities, then whether they are consciously aware of it or not, they may also confront a shift in their own most basic ontological assumptions.

2.2   Dynamic ontology

Due perhaps to the increasingly global scope of the business environment, or perhaps to the increasingly rapid pace of change enabled by information technologies, strategists have begun in the last decade or so to affirm the complexity of the business environment and question the static ontology outlined above. Abandoning the focus on static, predictable objects of scientific knowledge, a series of alternative conceptions have developed that characterize strategy content and processes as dynamic, emergent forms or patterns of activity.

For example, there is a stream of research inspired by complex adaptive systems theory that characterizes strategy *as* creativity (cf. Stacey, 1996). Based on this set of ontological assumptions, the primary activity of individual strategists involves a process that is 'like play in that it invites operation in the transitional zone of the mind, where reality and fantasy come together in the form of metaphors, analogies and images' (ibid. 280). A related stream of research has focused on strategy as a process of ecological adaptation (For example, Aldrich, 1979; De Geus, 1997) in which not only the environment and the organization change, but additionally the human capacity to make sense of this change also evolves over time. In this sense, strategic adaptation can be understood not simply as a behaviorist, stimulus/response mechanism, but *as* the reflective, social activity of sensemaking (cf. Weick, 1995) and organizational learning (for example, Cohen and Leventhal, 1990; Nonaka and Takeuchi, 1995; Argyris et al., 1995).

Perhaps the most provocative formulation of this ontological claim is the one that characterizes strategy *as* revolution (cf. Hamel, 1996), where the activity of the strategist involves systematically and deliberately innovating not only the organization's structure, but, more importantly, the mental models that organizational members use to make sense of their own activity. In turn, the formulation of this dynamic ontology that is most 'agnostic' on the question of the meaning and purpose of organizational transformation is the one that depicts strategy simply as a pattern (for example, Mintzberg, 1998b) in a stream of action. This agnosticism can, however, turn into cynicism when strategic planning processes are characterized as public relations (Mintzberg, 1994), and the articulation of strategic intent (Hamel and Prahalad, 1989) is characterized as a post-hoc rationalization that serves either (a) to present an appearance of rationality in order to assign responsibility for success or failure, or (b) to obscure the uncertainty of attaining any particular outcome in the future, and thereby to perpetuate the illusion of strategic management control.

But whether we accept or reject this hint of cynicism, and whether we prefer the descriptive metaphor of 'revolution' or 'creative play', the point here is simply that these various, alternative conceptions of strategy collectively represent a shift toward a 'dynamic ontology' in which unexpected change is a feature both of the business environment and of the human capacity to make sense of it. The static ontology presupposes that change occurs in accordance with laws and principles that do not change and can be known. By contrast, the dynamic ontology presupposes that the principles of change may also change, and moreover, that our knowledge of change is itself subject to unexpected change on an ongoing basis.[10]

This different set of presuppositions allows the field of strategic management to get over its so-called 'physics envy' and relinquish its aspiration to predict future events based on knowledge of necessary laws and principles. Of course, models that predict outcomes based on scientific analysis of the relationship between an organization and its environment can retain a certain degree of utility within this dynamic ontology. However, they cannot be mistaken for definitive, silver-bullet solutions to strategic problems, or for infallible methods of analysing problems. Instead, such models can be treated pragmatically as

---

[10] For an in-depth elaboration of both a dynamic ontology and epistemology see Roos, J. (2006) *Thinking from Within: A Hands-On Strategy Practice*, Basingstoke: Palgrave Macmillan, chapters 7–8.

provisional 'walking sticks'[11] that are cast aside as soon as they become a hindrance rather than an aid to action.[12]

But more importantly, this dynamic ontology has significant implications for how the challenge of preparedness is both defined and addressed strategically. Whereas preparedness refers in a static ontology to a state of affairs in which an organization has anticipated future events and developed capabilities sufficient to respond to them, in a dynamic ontology it refers to an unfolding process through which the 'external' environment and the 'internal' knowledge about the environment transform themselves recursively in relation to each other on an ongoing basis. More specifically, rather than an outcome variable that can be definitively produced or controlled for, the term 'preparedness' refers to a certain mode of relation or interaction between one complex system and another, where change in one system does not necessarily disrupt the other. From the perspective of strategic management, this mode of relation remains entirely contingent not

---

[11] Thomas, H. and Hafsi, T. (2005), 'The Field of Strategy: In Search of a Walking Stick,' *European Management Journal*, 23(5): 507–19.

[12] An objection may well arise on this point that, irrespective of the positivist ontology that guides the analysis of strategically-important dynamics in the firm and its context, the practicing manager deploys all such tools and techniques with a pragmatic spirit. In other words, we may anticipate that the strategist will recognize the limitations of predictive knowledge in the face of emergent change and concede, as per one of the most well-worn adages of strategy (attributed to von Clausewitz) that 'no plan survives contact with the enemy'. This objection, however, only defers our critique, splitting the issue into a debate, on one side, about the sources and functions of power, and on the other side, about the strategic importance of initial conditions and other context factors. In either case, however, we find that practicing managers (no less than military generals) remain quite unwilling to let go of the assumption that change can, to a certain extent, be anticipated and prepared for.

only on changing dynamics in the 'external' environment and in the 'internal' organization, but also at the level of the 'internal' assessment of the relationships among those various dynamics. In this sense, the 'strategic challenge of preparedness' calls not just for the development of knowledge and capabilities in response to an anticipated change, but, additionally, for the cultivation of patterns of mindful action that can continue to sustain the organization even in the face of unexpected change.

In more concrete terms, within the dynamic ontology the practice of strategy itself appears not just as an attempt, undertaken by senior leaders and expert analysts in an off-site location on a semi-annual basis, to close the perceived gap between the organization and its forecasted future reality. Additionally, the practice of strategy appears as any attempt, undertaken by anyone in the organization, to deal with a surprising or unexpected set of circumstances. Our question then becomes: *how, and to what extent, should these practices be changed in order to help the organization become more strategically prepared to deal with unexpected change?*

3.0
Defining the Problem

The ontological shift outlined above may, as such, correspond to a sequential process of historical development
(that is, as in the narrative cited above: *from* long-range
planning, *to* continuous adaptation) – though it may
additionally correspond to distinct, albeit contradictory
assumptions simultaneously held by individual members of a given organization or participants in a strategy
process. Moreover, the shift as we have portrayed it here
may not necessarily signal a stark, either/or choice. Indeed,
even if we proceed from a complex adaptive systems
perspective, pockets of stability can and do emerge, and
within these pockets regular patterns unfold that can
be anticipated with a significant degree of accuracy. And
yet at the same time, not only can these patterns change,
but our capacity to anticipate them can also change.
Thus by tracing this ontological shift, we have tried
simply to illustrate how the challenge of preparedness
takes shape in the context of contemporary strategic
management research and practice, and to show that the
difference between these two sets of assumptions raises a
series of questions that are of the utmost importance

to the practicing manager who deals with unexpected change.

If in fact we need 'to concern ourselves with process *and* content, statics *and* dynamics, constraint *and* inspiration, the cognitive *and* the collective, the planned *and* the learned, the economic *and* the political' (Mintzberg, 1998b: 373), then how exactly can people in organizations cultivate strategic preparedness in practice? If in fact 'strategy is something you *do* rather than something you *have* ... and this doing actually constitutes learning, not steering' (de Geus, 1997: 184, 189), then how can leaders guide the organization in a way that enables rather than constrains the cultivation of strategic preparedness? Finally, if in fact 'you can't see the end from the beginning' (Hamel, 1996: 81), then with what specific targets can strategists legitimately aspire to make the organization more prepared for the unexpected?

We will over the course of this book attempt to develop answers to each of these questions. For now, it is important to define the problem as we understand it.

At one level, the 'strategic challenge of preparedness' refers to a practical problem that arises whenever people in organizations deal with unexpected change. Phrased directly and subjectively: you are surprised, you don't know what to do, and that's the problem. As indicated above, this problem can confront people at all levels of the organizational hierarchy, from senior management and strategists, to line managers and production teams, to outsourced administrative staff. Moreover, this problem can arise irrespective of whether the consequences of the surprise event appear positive or negative at first glance. An unexpected growth opportunity can quickly become a financial disaster, as in the case of the so-called Internet economy – and conversely, an apparent disaster can quickly transform into an occasion to grow value through effective communications, as in the case of the Tylenol scare.[13] Finally, this problem can come in many different sizes, from a colleague's unexpected comment in a sales meeting, to the sudden shift of production capacity from Denmark to China, to the arrest of the CEO for fraud, to coordinated bomb attacks in the London public transportation system, and even to a tsunami that destroys coastal areas throughout southeast Asia or a hurricane that wreaks havoc on the Gulf Coast of the United States.

In each of these cases, and at each of these levels of scale, the problem of unexpected change signals a need for strategic preparedness. If we act in accordance with the assumptions of the static ontology, then we respond to this need by attempting to generate predictive knowledge about future events and to develop capabilities sufficient to handle all such events. But if we act in accordance with the dynamic ontology, and assume that unexpected change represents not a failure of strategy but instead a generic feature of the organizational environment, then we additionally respond to this need by attempting to cultivate patterns of mindful action that are robust enough to sustain the organization through large-scale, high-consequence changes, as well as everyday surprises.

In this light, the 'strategic challenge of preparedness' also refers to a theoretical problem that arises whenever people seek to identify those specific patterns of action that enable effective responses to unexpected change. This problem also becomes clear when phrased subjectively: you don't know how to describe how people can become more capable of dealing effectively with unexpected events. In this regard, the historical bias within the field of strategic

---

[13] In this oft-cited case story, the management response to a product scare had the effect of building greater trust in the organization and its products. Cf. Berge, T. (1990) *The First 24-Hours*, Cambridge, MA: Basil Blackwell, Inc; Fink, S. (1986) *Crisis Management: Planning for the Inevitable*, New York, NY: American Management Association.

management toward scientific models has resulted in a relative lack of general understanding about what managers actually do when they make strategy.[14] And because the practitioner-oriented management literature tends to offer either how-to checklists (that is, 'seven easy steps to success') or heroic personal testimonies (that is, 'I knew all along that my vision would produce success'), this lack appears even greater with respect to the specific problem of understanding how people act when they confront unexpected surprises. In any case, this lack signals a need for greater theoretical understanding of the strategic challenge of preparedness.

We therefore present this book as an attempt to build greater understanding about how people in organizations can, assuming a dynamic ontology, respond to the strategic challenge of preparedness.

---

[14] This lack is thankfully being addressed by the growing community of researchers focused on 'strategy-as-practice', of which more anon (cf. www.strategy-as-practice.org).

4.0
The Problem in Practice

Having just presented the strategic challenge of preparedness in the context of the history of strategic management, we now reflect carefully on what happens in practice when an unexpected change stretches beyond the limits of an organization's knowledge and response capability. We begin this process of reflection with a quote from a post-9/11 Council on Foreign Relations (CFR) report that succinctly enunciates the practical problem confronting strategists and organizational leaders who face the need for preparedness: 'We could spend our entire GNP on preparedness and still be unprepared.'[15]

This assessment of the post-9/11 US national security situation translates directly into a practical problem that appears intrinsic to the strategic challenge of preparedness. In short, whenever strategists 'think the unthinkable',[16]

---

[15] Council on Foreign Relations Independent Task Force (2003) *Emergency Responders: Drastically Underfunded, Dangerously Unprepared*, www.cfr.org.

[16] This phrase pervades the history of scenario planning, likely beginning with Hermann Kahn's work after the Second World War with the Rand Corporation and subsequently with the Hudson Institute. Following 9/11, the phrase has been cited repeatedly: cf. Mitroff, I. and Alpaslan, M. (2003).

then the range of 'thinkable' scenarios can quickly become
so great that the task of becoming adequately prepared
for them all stretches the limits of available resources.
This practical problem becomes acute when the resources
required to build up a response capacity (in anticipation
of a series of 'thinkable' events) within an existing organizational function exceed the sum total of the resources
that have previously sustained that function as such. And
in the most extreme case, the one addressed by the CFR
report, the cost of preparedness 'for the unthinkable' can
exceed the total revenue of the organization which
sought preparedness in the first place.

Let us consider this challenging strategic situation in
reference to a simple figure, where the *x*-axis represents the
level of threat, the *y*-axis represents the level of resources,
and the *a*-line represents the need for preparedness
(Figure 1).

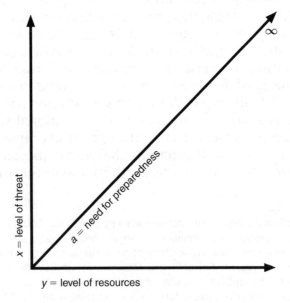

Figure 1   The infinite need for preparedness

This figure expresses the logic of the CFR claim that the level of threat faced by the United States may be so great that the need for preparedness extends far beyond the resources available to address it. We will explore this logic in the coming pages beginning with a more specific explanation of the various elements of Figure 1, including anecdotal illustrations of the *x*- and *y*-axes. We will then trace the implications of this logic, using practical examples to illustrate how the need for preparedness extends beyond the horizons of the unthinkable and the impossible. We identify two generic strategic options for organizations, as well as three tactical risks that are intrinsic to these two options. We then argue that as organizational leaders pursue strategic action in view of these tactical risks, they enter 'zones of acceptable risk', where they cannot rely on existing knowledge or capabilities, but instead can *only justify certain actions or courses of action by invoking ethical values*. In this way, the CFR claim will lead us toward a concept of inter-subjective, ethically-grounded 'practical wisdom' – distinct from objective, scientifically-grounded 'knowledge' – for organizations confronting the strategic challenge of preparedness.

4.1 The infinite need for preparedness

The United States Department of Homeland Security's (DHS) 'Homeland Security Advisory System' has received a great deal of public attention since it was introduced. In this system, levels of risk are differentiated visually in accordance with different colors, from green ('low risk of terrorist attack') to blue ('general risk of terrorist attack') to yellow ('significant risk of terrorist attack') to orange ('high risk of terrorist attack') and finally to red ('severe risk of terrorist attack'). The system functions in such a way as to provide information and guidance to all interested parties, including specific regional and industrial sectors of interest, and it is 'binding on the executive branch and suggested, although voluntary, to other levels of government and the private sector.' As an illustration of how this system works in practice, as of August 1, 2004, 'The United States Government raised the threat level to Code Orange for the financial services sector in New York City, northern New Jersey and Washington, D.C. The rest of the country remains at Code Yellow.'[17]

While it is not immediately apparent to an interested web surfer how DHS analysts are assessing the risk associated with these threats, they do refer to a series of guiding questions ('To what degree is the threat information credible? To what degree is the threat information corroborated? To what degree is the threat specific and/or imminent? How grave are the potential consequences of the threat').[18] For the purposes of demonstration, however, we can cite this 'security system' as an illustration of the 'level of threat' that serves as our *x*-axis in Figure 1.

Another illustration of how this axis might be construed at an organizational level of scale is the practice of rating credit risk by institutions like Standard and Poor's, or Moody's. These systems serve as early warning indicators of potential threats to creditors, and are thus analogous to the DHS advisory system. At a national level of

---

[17] These two quotes appear on the DHS website: http://www.dhs.gov/dhspublic/display?theme = 29 (accessed on 11 October 2004).

[18] The relative significance of these factors could of course vary widely and remain subject to interpretation. To wit: an estimated 50% likelihood that a teenage terrorist in the Philippines will hack the DHS website tomorrow should obviously not represent the same 'level of threat' as the .001% chance that Al Qaeda will detonate a 'suitcase nuke' in a metropolitan center. In this sense, irrespective of whether the DHS security system registers orange today or yellow tomorrow, it remains open to question whether, in the words of the 9-11 Commission Report, 'the system is [still] blinking red' (254).

scale, attempts to assess the relative competitiveness of countries (as undertaken by the International Institute for Management Development (IMD) and the World Economic Forum (WEF)) provide a means of informing the business community about various risk factors that might impact operations. And at a more individual level of scale, in-company efforts to map and categorize employee competencies can also be seen as a way to inform decision-makers about the levels of risk that pertain to the intellectual capital currently residing within the organization. Thus as we focus on the logic of the CFR claim, each of these examples provides an illustration of how the 'level of threat' can be assessed, and how that assessment becomes relevant when people make decisions and take actions in response to the need for preparedness.

As for the y-axis in Figure 1, the 'level of resources' refers to the sum total of resources available to an organization as it confronts the need for preparedness. Again, the CFR report provides a first illustration of this axis, as it estimates the resources available to the United States as it confronts terrorism in terms of the gross national product (GNP). At another level of scale, this y-axis might be analysed in terms of the profit margin, the operating budget, or even the net present assets of an organization – but again, these examples provide specific illustrations of the generic 'level of resources' represented by the y-axis.

Of course, such 'resources' need not be seen simply as stockpiles of available assets. Recall, for example, the movement beginning in the mid-1990s that sought to visualize and even measure the value creation potential in organizations that could hardly be captured in the balance sheet. The notion of 'intellectual capital' referred to the many 'hidden' assets of organizations, like systems and knowledge, as analogous to material assets, like buildings and machines, in terms of their value. Eventually, this balance sheet based view of intellectual capital evolved into a focus on how these assets were *utilized* to create value (cf. Roos et al., 1997; Roos and Roos, 1998). Rather than focusing on stable 'assets' the evolving idea was to understand and improve intellectual capital *flows* among all kinds of material and immaterial resources in organizations. It is in this sense that the *y*-axis in Figure 1 could also be conceptualized in terms of 'resource flows' or 'resource utilization capacity' – though again, we intend these generic characterizations to remain analytically meaningful across different levels of scale.

In any case, by defining the two axes in this generic way, our point is not to quibble over the methods of analysis whereby levels of threat and levels of resources are to be estimated or established. Instead, we wish to indicate at the level of basic assumptions (i) how the need for preparedness is theoretically infinite, while the capacity to respond to that need in practice remains *limited* by what is thinkable and possible for organizations, and (ii) how change on either axis impacts the need for preparedness.

The propositions expressed by Figure 1 are therefore as follows:

- if we increase the level of threat, then the need for preparedness also increases;
- and in turn, if the need for preparedness increases, then additional resources are required by organizations in order to be prepared.[19]

---

[19] We can also speculate as to whether the converse may also be true, namely whether an increase in the level of resources causes the need for preparedness to increase, and whether the threat level would, in turn, rise in proportion. This proposition seems reasonable in principle to an extent – for example, if a property has greater value, then the insurance premium to insure it is greater. The question of whether such property is actually at greater *risk* would seem to depend on the context. In any case, this logical proposition seems to inform the debatable line of political argument that maintains that 'the terrorists hate us because they are jealous of our way of life'.

We should note that this representation of the practical problem confronting strategists and organizational leaders rests on the assumption that the threat potential is asymmetric, a concept defined in the 1998 Strategic Assessment published by the United States National Defense University as follows:

> Put simply, asymmetric threats or techniques are a version of not 'fighting fair,' which can include *the use of surprise in all its operational and strategic dimensions* and the use of weapons in ways unplanned by the United States. Not fighting fair also includes the prospect of an opponent designing a strategy that fundamentally alters the terrain on which a conflict is fought. (179; our italics)

In accordance with this definition of asymmetry, any 'unplanned' event in which an organization is 'surprised' and finds itself on a 'fundamentally altered terrain' appears first (whether in reality or as a hypothetical scenario) as something previously 'unthinkable'.

With the benefit of hindsight, history appears filled with examples of how companies missed opportunities as the landscape shifted in unplanned ways that rendered their previous initiatives fundamentally obsolete. For example, Apple's innovative but bulky Newton handheld organizer, launched in 1993, was rendered obsolete by Palm a few years later. Similarly, installation of the innovative Minitel network in virtually all households in France pre-dated the Internet, but once the Internet became available, its adoption was delayed in France by the presence of the alternative technology. Beyond technology, the unanticipated criminal prosecution of organizational leaders who had previously been worshipped for their innovative ideas and ways of working has fundamentally shifted the terrain of leadership and corporate governance in recent years.

We can therefore say, precisely in view of (relatively mundane) organizational illustrations such as these, that the practical problem outlined above takes shape as strategists and organizational leaders seek to become more prepared for such surprises by thinking the unthinkable. As they then face an asymmetric threat potential, they realize that the need for preparedness is much greater than they had anticipated, so great in fact that it extends beyond their organization's capacity to respond, no matter how many material or intellectual resources may be available.

4.2　The unthinkable

As we continue to trace the implications of the CFR claim that 'we could spend our entire GNP and still be

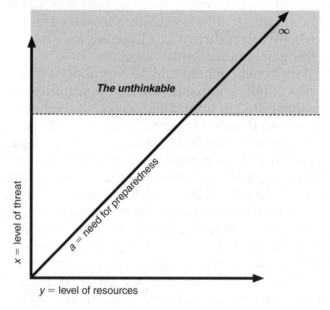

Figure 2　The unthinkable

unprepared', we find that movement or distance on the
x-axis, defined generically as 'level of threat', can be
assessed in relative terms with respect to a horizon or
limit condition, 'the unthinkable'.

The dotted line in Figure 2 represents not only the
limits of what can be known or predicted scientifically,
but additionally the limits of what might be imagined.[20]
In this way, we deliberately sidestep the issue of whether
the level of threat is 'real' or 'perceived' and open up the
possibility that the threat might be 'enacted' through
the social process of speculative reasoning itself.[21] But if
for the time being we adopt an agnostic position on this
difficult epistemological question, then based on the
assumption of an asymmetric threat potential, it appears
that the limits of the thinkable are recognized most com-
monly when they are surpassed in the experience of
surprise.

The 9–11 Commission Report has famously analyzed
the surprise element of the 9–11 attacks as evidence of a
'failure of imagination'. Following this analysis, imagination would appear precisely as the individual (and
organizational) capacity to think what is unthinkable. The
Commission Report claims specifically that '*it is therefore
crucial to find a way of routinizing, even bureaucratizing, the*

---

[20] Those individuals (especially the ones who participated in the
Aspen Institute Socrates Seminar in the summer of 2004) who have
not yet given up on becoming prophets provide an illustration of the
perennial futurist's dream of knowledge for which no empirical proof
can yet exist.

[21] In this respect, the question of what is thinkable or unthinkable
involves both epistemological reflections on cognitive blind spots, as
well as psychological reflections on the affective dynamics that pertain to the foundational presuppositions on which many strategists
and decision-makers operate.

exercise of the imagination' (344).[22] Whatever the likelihood of discovering such an apparently paradoxical routine may be, it may only be possible to recognize the failure of imagination with hindsight. And of course, as is tragically evident in the apparent disconnect throughout early 2001 between Richard Clarke's counter-terrorism organization and the Bush administration, imagining a scenario is quite different from doing something effectively to forestall it, or to prepare for its inevitability.[23]

The challenge is similar for company leaders. As much as scenario learning can help to broaden an organization's strategic perspective, the inherent problem is that such processes necessarily involve a reduction of the number of uncontrollable variables in the interest of developing future scenarios that appear plausible. But reality, with its possible permutations, frequently refuses to respect our notions of plausibility. It is one thing to vary the oil price and see what happens, but quite another to compound

---

[22] Our research suggests that by changing the process of strategy formulation to include playful modes of intentionality as well as three-dimensional media for expression, the content of strategy can also change to become more imaginative (see Roos, Victor and Statler, 2004). Subsequent research suggests that this effect is escalated when the playful activity also includes drama techniques to encourage the state of spontaneity, which in turn boosts intuition and improvisation (Roos, 2006).

[23] This point is particularly salient for example in the global warming debates. Whereas some scientific evidence places causal significance on factors which are clearly subject to human control (for example, CFCs, deforestation, and so on), other evidence cites relevant factors which cannot possibly be altered by human intervention (such as sunspot cycles). In an excellent example of 'imagining the unthinkable' Peter Schwartz and the Global Business Network (GBN) submitted a report to the Pentagon in 2003 which argued that preparedness for abrupt climate change was a matter of national security (cf. http://-www.ems.org/climate/pentagon_climatechange.pdf – accessed 10/12/2004).

that simplified picture with additional uncertainties, like an outbreak of a nasty, incurable avian flu pandemic, a tsunami wiping out the Tokyo bay area, a 'dirty bomb' in St Paul's Cathedral, or an unexpected Chinese invasion of Taiwan. The difficulty gets worse if we add to this list a few somewhat 'less plausible' uncertainties, like an amateur astronomer discovering a Shoemaker-Levy-like comet heading our way for an encounter in 23 years, or the sudden revelation that US President George Bush may have worn a radio transmitter that supplied him with answers to questions during the televised campaign debates in 2004.

The point in articulating such implausible events is to illustrate that whether the surprise occurs in reference to a real event or an imagined scenario – that is, whether the limits of the thinkable are confronted *pre* or *post facto* – the practical challenge for organizational leaders arises whenever a particular event becomes thinkable in such a way as to make the need for preparedness seem difficult, if not impossible to overcome.

4.3   The impossible

In turn, distance or movement on the *y*-axis, defined generically as 'level of resources', can be similarly assessed in relative terms with respect to a horizon or limit condition, 'the impossible'.

The second dotted line in Figure 3 thus represent the limits of what can be done, or the total exhaustion of the practical means for action. The CFR report sketches this limit in dramatic terms with reference to the GNP – re-phrased, their assertion is that public- and private-sector organizations in the US could exhaust *all available means* without achieving the strategic objective of preparedness. This characterization of the limit of the possible dodges the question of whether human action is ultimately

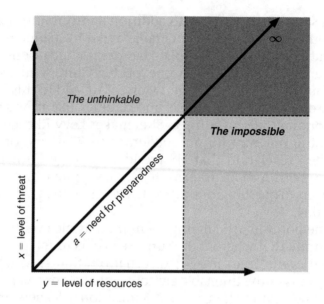

Figure 3 The impossible

limited by necessity (that is, metaphorically put, without fuel, an engine cannot run) or by proclivity (that is, without hope, the will to survive is lost).[24]

But in any case, just as the limits of the thinkable are confronted in the experience of surprise, the limits of possibility are confronted ultimately in the experience of death,[25] or perhaps less dramatically (and more proximally), in the experience of failure or defeat. Of course, the significance of failure in organizational contexts

---

[24] As we will see later, the human ethical situation involves a confrontation with both of these limits – in a phrase offered by Martha Nussbaum, we exist 'between luck and ethics' (2001).
[25] In this regard, we are indebted to *Aporias*, the text in which philosopher Jacques Derrida dealt with the paradoxical 'possibility of impossibility' that appears when other people die in the experiential terms of a 'death which is in each case mine'.

depends on one's point of view. From an economic perspective, the failure of a business can be considered a natural phenomenon, with positive effects for the market – while from a management perspective, the failure of a business is more personal and more traumatic, involving bankruptcy or foreclosure, a termination of effort and intentions.

In the context of strategy, then, we suggest that organizations fail terminally when they exhaust their available capacity to utilize resources. But when it comes to preparedness, this capacity can only be estimated in direct proportion to the strategic question: 'prepared for what?' As we noted above, the history of strategic management thinking exhibits a general trend from a static ontology toward a dynamic ontology of change. In the context of this trend, the singular event of the 9-11 terrorist attacks has brought the challenge of preparedness to the top of the leadership agenda. At the same time, it (as well as subsequent attacks in Madrid, Istanbul and London) has broadened the spectrum of 'thinkable' possibilities and thereby increased the variety as well as the level of resources required for organizations to avoid failure. This variety is, however, driven not just by the fact that the preparedness field[26] involves many different organizations with many different objectives, nor just by the fact that so many different threats are 'thinkable'. The variety of resources required to avoid failure is instead driven by the simple fact that preparedness, as a concept, directs our attention to an empty set (that is, Prepared for what? What is the unexpected?) that in principle remains infinitely subject to variation.

To be sure, this theoretically infinite variation is always constrained by patterns of convention and circumstance. The boy scout should be nominally prepared to help an

---

[26]'Field' should here and throughout this book be understood following Bourdieu's conceptualization (1990).

old lady cross the street, or to cope if lost in the woods without food. A national government should be nominally prepared to protect the interests of its citizens in the face of internal or external security threats. Most broadly, any organization should be nominally prepared to continue operations even when confronted with unexpected change. The practical problem faced by leaders is that, as answers to the 'prepared for what?' question proliferate, the need for preparedness can rise beyond the organization's capacity to respond.[27]

So then, what can they do?

---

[27] We here acknowledge and sidestep the additional problem in bureaucratic institutions that pertains to the bias for following 'the plan' until long after the resource capacity has been overwhelmed.

5.0
Dealing with the Practical Problem

For organizations that find themselves approaching the horizons of the unthinkable and the impossible, two generic strategies are available: either (i) measures can be taken to diminish or mitigate the level of threat (Figure 4), or (ii) measures can be taken to extend the available resources and/or to optimize the organization's resource utilization capacity (Figure 5). In practice, these strategies will almost always be blended in some way or another, but we will analyse them here separately at first in the interest of clarity.

5.1 Strategy 1 – lower the level of threat

The mitigation of the threat potential is the first generic strategy that organizations can pursue in response to the need for preparedness. As expressed in Figure 4, the logical proposition driving this strategy is that by lowering the level of threat, the need for preparedness would decrease. And if such a strategy were definitively to achieve its goal, the need for preparedness would be decreased to such an extent that it would be possible for an organization to respond adequately and effectively to all thinkable events.

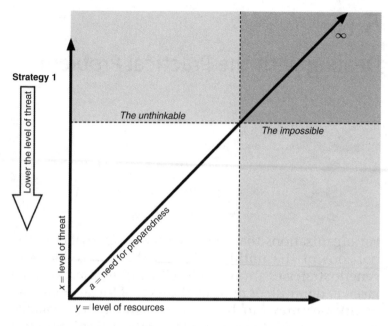

Figure 4   Strategy 1 – lower the level of threat

To support this strategic objective, leaders can of course apply a series of risk management tactics, including: making smaller investments, developing prototypes, using several suppliers, reducing dependency on a few big clients, building processes and systems that reduce dependency on certain individuals, lobbying regulators, rallying the public's support, protecting intellectual property, complying with private-sector disaster and catastrophe preparedness standards, and so on. They may even seek to define themselves out of the risk category by deciding that they should not be involved with, responsible for, or interested in certain businesses or actions.

In any case, the generic advantages of pursuing Strategy 1 include the fact that evidence of actions taken can be relatively easy to demonstrate to stakeholders, especially when the threat is clear and distinct, when it can be definitively neutralized (for example, through the capture of an adversary). Furthermore, even when the threat is less than clear, the proactive nature of the strategic action can inspire hope and confidence within the organization. However, Strategy 1 has several generic disadvantages as well. For example, the asymmetric threat potential means that even a vastly diminished threat can still have unforeseen and even disastrous consequences, that is, the much-discussed 'butterfly effect'. Moreover, the tactical effectiveness of specific threat mitigation actions can only be demonstrated in two ways, either (i) by indications of events that might have happened but didn't because of preparedness measures (for example, the foiled plot), or (ii) by evidence of actual events having relatively minimized impact because of preparedness measures (for example, the disaster's impacts were contained). And based on a dynamic ontology, the limits of the thinkable can always shift again.

Of course, an organization working to implement Strategy 1 would ideally discover a silver bullet that neutralizes the threat with great efficiency and at minimal cost. In practice, however, such solutions are difficult to identify, and even in cases when they can be identified, the means required for research and development can be excessive.[28] In such situations, organizational leaders may find themselves compelled to pursue a second generic strategy involving the optimization of available resources.

5.2   Strategy 2 – optimize resources

The optimization of existing resources is a second generic strategy that can be pursued by organizations in response

---

[28] An extreme case illustration of the excessive (financial and moral) costs associated with the 'silver bullet' strategy can be found in the Manhattan Project.

to the infinite need for preparedness. At a certain point (that is, approaching the limits of the possible), an organization cannot simply borrow more money, or conscript more labor, but instead must use the limited resources available to it more effectively. Phrased in colloquial terms, if the organization cannot work harder, then it must learn to work smarter – this endeavor is captured in the term 'resource optimization' and efficiency.[29]

As expressed in Figure 5, the proposition driving Strategy 2 is that by optimizing the available resources, by being more efficient, the current levels of resource utilization would decrease, and although the need for preparedness would not necessarily decrease, the capacity for response to the need would be extended. If such a strategy were definitively to achieve its goal, then the organization would develop an effective capacity to respond adequately and effectively to all thinkable events.

Among private sector organizations, specific tactics designed to optimize resource use (and thereby to drive down the level of resources required to respond to the need for preparedness) include all efforts to work smarter and be more parsimonious with available resources, including: strategic planning; process re-engineering; just-in-time manufacturing; TQM; enterprise resource planning (ERP); supply chain management; and intellectual capital systems. Within the field of preparedness, this same strategic principle is illustrated by the 'all-hazards' approach, as it guides practice and tactics in different functional areas, including: enterprise risk management,

---

[29] Related concepts include: recycling, conservation, efficiency improvement, and so on. See also 'creative recombination' as addressed by Eric Abrahamson in *Change without Pain: How Managers Can Overcome Initiative Overload, Organizational Chaos and Employee Burnout.* (2004). Cambridge: Harvard University Press.

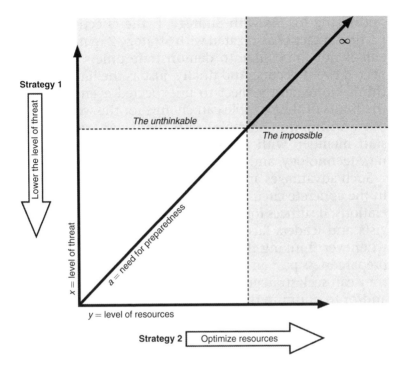

Figure 5   Strategy 2 – optimize resources

business continuity planning, emergency preparedness, security, and so on.

Like Strategy 1, Strategy 2 has several generic advantages. In principle, organizations benefit from efficiency in any case, so optimization should have positive implications irrespective of whether the thinkable event happens or not. Additionally, resource optimization takes place at the level of the everyday behaviors and interactions of people in organizations, so its implications may similarly be readily perceptible by members of the organization. However, Strategy 2 also has generic disadvantages. In practice, the optimization of resources totally depends on what purpose, goal or hypothetical scenario one is optimizing for. As with Strategy 1, the effectiveness of particular tactics associated with Strategy 2 remains difficult if not impossible to demonstrate unless an unexpected event occurs. And finally, just as the limits of the thinkable remain subject to unexpected events, so too the limits of the possible can change for the worse without warning (for example, with the departure of a key staff member, with the discovery or deployment of a new technology, and so on).

Such advantages and disadvantages must be evaluated in the concrete circumstances for action. For our considerations, it suffices for now to acknowledge that as strategists and leaders face the practical problem that arises whenever thinking the unthinkable drives the need for preparedness past an organization's capacity to respond, they can seek strategically to mitigate the level of threat, and/or to optimize the available resources.

6.0
Facing Tactical Risks

As noted above, these two formally distinct preparedness strategies may be blended to such an extent that they become indistinct in practice. Indeed, we suggest that any particular tactical action should ideally advance or contribute to both of these strategies at the same time. Moreover, organizations should ideally be able to strike a balance between these two strategies and become more prepared for future change in such a way as simultaneously to extend their operational effectiveness in the present.[30]

From a governance perspective, these two 'ideals' can function as evaluative criteria for preparedness-related investments: for example, to what extent does a particular course of action (i) involve *both* threat mitigation *and* resource optimization, and (ii) serve *both* to improve production in the present *and* to develop the capacity to respond to unexpected change in the future. However, even if we can affirm the ultimate, perpetual motion

---

[30] There is a related line of questioning about how the investment and attention currently being paid to catastrophe preparedness might be focused in such a way as to enable organizations to deal more effectively on an everyday basis with emergent change. We suggest that this important issue can be addressed most effectively through dialogue among communities of practice.

fantasy of strategic management as the practice of ensuring the long-term survival and growth of the organization without compromising its short-term operational health, we must still confront a less-than-fantastic reality.

Indeed, as organizations find themselves approaching the limits of what is thinkable or possible, every attempt to strike a balance between these two strategies involves a distinct set of tactical risks. At best, striking this balance involves a confrontation with the law of diminishing returns (Figure 6). At worst, organizations find themselves confronted with counter-productive scenarios involving blowback (Figure 7) and squander (Figure 8).

6.1 Tactical risk 1 – diminishing returns

The first, most basic risk faced by leaders at the limits of the thinkable and the possible is that any given tactic involves at best a hedge against unpredictable future events. Given the contingent and provisional nature of such hedges, and given the manifest diversity of thinkable event scenarios, it might seem logical to assume that if one hedge were good, then twenty would be better. And yet, even as one hedging tactic or several may marginally decrease the level of threat or optimize the resource utilization, as these tactics accumulate, then at a certain point an organization risks confronting the law of diminishing returns (Figure 6).[31]

---

[31] Cf. W. J. Spillman and E. Lang, *The Law of Diminishing Returns* (1924). Generically phrased, this law states that if one factor of production is increased while the others remain constant, the overall returns will relatively decrease after a certain point. Specifically translated to the present context, we might say provocatively that while the invasion of Afghanistan increased 'returns' by making the US more prepared for terrorist attacks, the invasion of Iraq is debatable in its consequences. We can of course only speculate, but it would seem that neoconservative proposals to invade Syria, Iran and/or North Korea would (even if we grant sufficient military resources) diminish returns and risk making the US less prepared against terrorist threats.

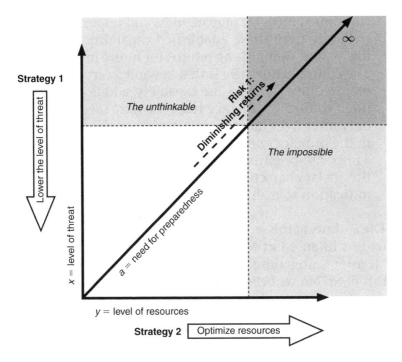

Figure 6   Tactical risk 1 – diminishing returns

In the logic of Figure 6, when organizations invest time and money in Strategy 1 and/ or Strategy 2 in an effort to respond to the need for preparedness, they face the risk of diminishing returns, where at a certain point additional investment on the margin contributes less and less to the strategic objective, and begins instead to detract from it.

The cruel implications of this law for the preparedness field are stated quite clearly in a research report distributed by the Canada's Office for Critical Infrastructure Protection and Emergency Preparedness:

> Experience in Canada demonstrates a diversity of response capabilities and readiness within the institutional organizations responsible for emergencies.

Continued focus on preparedness and response follows naturally from these established capabilities, but will likely show diminishing returns for future investments. The contradiction here is that beyond a certain level of preparedness and response capability, additional investment to further enhance response may save lives, but only after lives have been lost and property damaged in the primary impact. These underlying limitations of a response-oriented approach have drawn attention to the social character of disasters, and the potential of mitigation to realize loss reductions.[32]

The authors of this report identify the point of diminishing returns in an effort to underscore the need for pro-active 'disaster mitigation' strategies. We similarly recognize this need, but we believe that although Strategy 1 outlined above involves 'mitigation', it does not therefore avoid the risk of diminishing returns. In fact, it seems clear that the law of diminishing returns provides an ultimate horizon for any and all forms of 'enterprise risk management' – namely, where the effort to manage the risk becomes marginally less effective. This risk of diminishing returns appears endemic to the preparedness 'production system' itself.

The point at which this risk becomes relevant to a particular set of organizational activities can, however, vary significantly, depending primarily on the importance of 'returns' on investment. Indeed, we can demonstrate with reference to one simple, best case scenario – no future terrorist attacks – how the risk of diminishing returns affects public and private sector organizations differently.

In the public interest, the logic of spending money on preparedness without any hope of direct returns on the

---

[32] http://www.ocipep.gc.ca/research/resactivites/disMit/en_mitigat/ NEWTON_1995D014_e.pdf – accessed 10/12/2004

investment should be quite familiar, however perverse it may at first appear: for example, the Cold War notion that 'we are developing and maintaining a nuclear arsenal with the great hope that we never have to use it', and so on. This longstanding tradition of deterrence suggests that extensive preparedness measures should be taken without question, largely in deference to the scale of potentially negative consequences for the public interest. In the organizational context of US national security, for example, the question of whether returns on investment begin to diminish after the (n)th dollar in the DHS budget, or after the $(1 + n)$th, seems to matter hardly at all.

On the other hand, it is already painfully clear that for private sector organizational leaders with quarterly targets and annual profit margins in mind, it can be a struggle to justify investments in preparedness-related measures that contribute little or nothing by their very design to the bottom line.[33] Indeed, to the extent corporate decision-makers may feel a general reluctance to invest in preparedness-related measures for the organization, it may be that they consider the entire preparedness effort to be *de facto* beyond the point of diminishing returns.[34]

As an illustration of the risk of diminishing returns, consider the now-distant history of Y2K. In retrospect, some organizations felt that the Y2K scare was a scam designed to scare IT managers into spending on systems

---

[33] In this regard, it remains the role of the state to provide the private sector with incentives and penalties that compel compliance in the interest of public safety issues no less significant than continuity of operations for the government itself.

[34] It may, of course, be a question of diminishing returns *for the CEO*, given the relatively short-term time horizons and narrow self-interest encouraged by corporate compensation plans. In such cases, the preparedness investment is simply deferred in hope that 'it won't happen on my watch'.

upgrades. For other organizations, the Y2K systems upgrade had immediate and demonstrable impacts on organizational productivity. But in both of these cases, the null scenario that nothing catastrophic actually happened to information systems on January 1, 2000, meant that organizations faced a high risk of diminishing returns. Indeed, at what point was investment in Y2K compliance sufficient? Should the assessments conducted by, or cited in sales meetings by IT service companies be trusted on the matter? What percentage of the IT budget brought diminished returns in 1999? Would that percentage be different if something catastrophic had actually happened? And finally: could these questions be answered to provide guidance for IT-related investments in business continuity made in response to the strategic challenge of preparedness today?

As difficult as it may be for organizational leaders and organizational scholars to answer such questions definitively, the law of diminishing returns represents the best-case tactical risk confronted by organizations as they balance strategies at the limits of what is thinkable and possible. A number of worst-case risks exist as well. In particular, we wish to address two distinct risks that a particular tactic will have unintended effects that directly contradict and subvert the strategic objective it was designed to serve.

6.2   Tactical risk 2 – blowback

Actions can sometimes bring about deleterious, 'blowback' effects that inadvertently increase the level of threat faced by the organization (cf. Figure 7).

In the logic of Figure 7, as organizations pursue either Strategy 1 or Strategy 2, they utilize tactics that have the inadvertent and unforeseen effect of raising the level of threat, and thus increasing rather than decreasing the

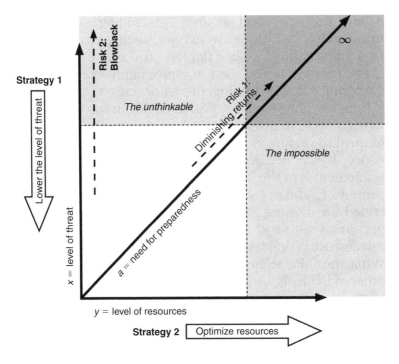

Figure 7   Tactical risk 2 – blowback

need for preparedness. As an illustration of blowback, consider the following account of the Abu Ghraib scandal, as told in the *New Yorker* by Pulitzer Prize-winning journalist Seymour Hersh.[35]

A 'black' special access program (SAP) was set up by the Pentagon in early 2002 in Afghanistan to go after Bin Laden and Mullah Omar. A number of people were 'read into' the program, and designated 'extra judicial' in their actions, so they could pursue their objectives by any

----

[35] Hersh has explored these issues in more detail in his 2004 book, *Chain of Command: The Road from 9/11 to Abu Ghraib*. HarperCollins.

means necessary and available, including the use of unorthodox techniques to extract intelligence information from captured Taliban fighters. And although extreme measures were in fact used, the program was effective in gathering valuable intelligence information.

Roughly one year later, US-led coalition forces were up to their necks in insurgency in Iraq. As a method of trying to quell the insurgency by gathering more effective intelligence, it was decided to extend the SAP program and implement it in the Baghdad prisons. Groups of operators came to Baghdad to implement the program, and they ended up training and working with the regular Army personnel who had standing orders to provide military intelligence operators with standard coordination support. While the SAP operators remained above prosecution, these other individuals, including the poor 'hillbillies' from West Virginia whose pictures have subsequently been broadcast around the world, had no such immunity to prosecution.

As these two groups of people began to turn the thumbscrews on the 'fruit vendors' and the 'brothers-in-law', pretty soon good intelligence was generated that assisted the coalition authority with the suppression of the Iraqi insurgency. But of course, even though the short-term tactical objective was obtained and better intelligence was secured, the blowback effect became increasingly relevant as the story unfolded. The unintended, negative effects worsened as the public became aware not only of abuse, but of various attempts within the US administration both to mitigate the negative implications of the abuse and, at the same time, to justify the program and its objectives.

Among the policy leaders, the strategic logic of justification for the program was that 'we don't have time to consult with the logistics planners, risk analysts, deal with planning and so forth. Instead, we have an urgent need to get actionable intelligence, so we need to make a judgment, draw the line and just go for it.'

But in hindsight, such justifications of that relatively small, special project pale in comparison to the blowback effects that its implementation has had. Indeed, while the scandal has subsequently diminished as an object of attention of the international news media, its implications in the minds of Iraqi and other Middle Eastern people threatens to overshadow the insurgency itself as a factor that disrupts not only the organizational development project in Iraq, but also the spread of democracy and the American 'way of life' throughout the Middle East.

The point of this story for our purposes is that, if Hersh's account is correct, actions were taken by the US government that sought to lower the level of threat but instead had the inadvertent effect of increasing it. 'Blowback' describes those situations in which a given strategy has the effect of driving up rather than lowering the level of threat. In turn, this increased level of threat requires additional resources from an organization in order to respond to the need for preparedness.

Blowback is a sadly common phenomenon among private-sector organizations dealing with the uncertainty of the business environment. For example, on November 21, 2001 the European Union imposed record fines against drug companies that had colluded to fix the price of vitamins. Evidence gathered by US investigators showed that the companies dictated all aspects of vitamin sales, and that the cartel's executives met annually to fix a budget in an arrangement known by some participants as 'Vitamins Inc'. Eight companies were fined 855.2 million euros for what the EU antitrust officials described as the most damaging series of cartels the commission had ever investigated. Hoffman-La Roche of Switzerland received the largest fine, 462 million euros, for being the prime mover and main beneficiary of the cartel. A few years earlier Roche had agreed to pay a $500 million fine to settle charges by the US Justice Department. French group Aventis (at that time known as Rhône-Poulenc) was also involved in the cartel, but was granted full immunity because it helped the Commission with decisive information.[36] In a 19 August 1999 press release, the US Department of Justice described how a senior Roche executive, who pleaded guilty, had coordinated the cartel. From spring 1991 until February 1999, this executive engaged with-counterparts at BASF, Rhône-Poulenc, and other co-conspirators in agreeing to: (i) fix and raise prices on vitamins and vitamin premixes; (ii) allocate volume of sales and market shares of such vitamins; (iii) divide contracts to supply vitamin premixes to customers by rigging the bids for those contracts; and (iv) participate in meetings and conversations to monitor and enforce adherence to the agreed-upon prices and market shares. In public sources it is said the Roche people carefully recorded these discussions and agreements just like any other business dealings. As Gary R. Spratling, the Antitrust Division's Deputy Assistant Attorney General for criminal enforcement, said in a 19 August 2000 press release: 'As a member of Hoffmann-La Roche's Executive Committee at the time of his involvement, (he) put the full weight of legitimacy behind the company's involvement in the most pervasive international cartel ever uncovered.' In the US case, four executives of Roche and BASF received fines and prison sentences for their role in the price fixing and subsequent cover up. Assistant Attorney General Joel I. Klein of the US Justice Department said, 'Without the active support and participation of these executives, the vitamin conspiracy never would have been implemented, let alone in such an organized and effective manner.'[37] The detailed

---

[36] The other cartel members included BASF (Germany), Rhône-Poulenc/Aventis (France), Slovey Pharmaceuticals BV (Netherlands), Merck KGaA (Germany), Daiichi Pharmaceutical Co. Ltd (Japan), Eisai Co. Ltd (Japan), and Takeda Chemical Industries Ltd (Japan).

records turned out to be very helpful to investigators, and helped them quickly unravel the cartel and the key individuals' roles in it. All told the careful preparations to ensure the effectiveness of the cartel, and thereby, to diminish the level of risk posed by change in the market for vitamins, resulted in blowback, with at least one direct effect of sending the responsible executives to jail.

These various illustrations allow us to see blowback as a risk that organizations must face as they respond to the need for preparedness either by seeking to reduce the level of threat (Strategy 1) or by optimizing the available resources (Strategy 2). For our purposes, it is important to see blowback as a risk that organizations can manage, but which may nevertheless come as an unpleasant surprise.

6.3   Tactical risk 3 – squander

In addition to blowback, organizations additionally face the tactical risk that their strategic efforts to become more prepared will result inadvertently in the squander of resources (cf. Figure 8), thus lowering the limits of what is possible to accomplish.

In the logic of Figure 8, as organizations pursue generic Strategy 1 and/or Strategy 2, they inadvertently squander resources in such a way as to reduce their capacity to respond to the need for preparedness. As an illustration of this situation, consider the following story about preparedness-related budget allocation processes in the United States.

A number of news reports provided details about the strife between the Governor's Office in the state of New York, as well as one of New York City Mayor Bloomberg's deputies, and legislators and government

---

[37] Source: Press release from US Justice Department, 6 April 2000: http://www.useu.be/ISSUES/vita0406.html

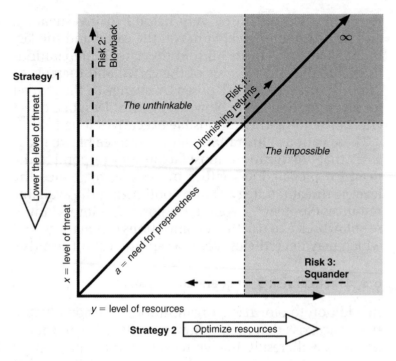

Figure 8   Tactical risk 3 – squander

officials from other states during 2003 and 2004. According to these reports, the people of Utah received the highest per capita federal allocation of homeland security dollars. So the New York position was essentially that this allocation process was unfair, a classic example of pork barrel legislation. For their part, the Utah government officials acknowledged the apparent discrepancy but argued somewhat paradoxically that actually the challenge is that the terrorists will always strike where we least expect it, and Utah is where you would least expect it. Also, for the people of Utah, it was important to acknowledge some of the very large national security installations out there that are potentially subject to attack, in addition to other relevant factors.[38]

The response from New York was that while it may be true that the potential risk of terrorist threat to the people of Utah is great, we have to differentiate potential targets in terms of their symbolic visibility. Furthermore, if we acknowledge that it is possible to expect what we least expect, then it's also possible to expect that a high-visibility target would be strategically most effective. Terrorists have demonstrated that it's possible to attack New York City, so there's no reason to think they wouldn't do it again. In fact, the terrorists may just be waiting for the right opportunity, and in the meantime, if we pass too much money on to Utah, we might as well invite Al Qaeda to come back to New York.

Stepping back a bit to take a strategic perspective on this debate, but granting that we could spend our entire GNP on preparedness and still be unprepared, what exactly do we want to buy for the people of Utah? What do we want to buy for the people of New York? What is the relative value on a national level of those state-level collective interests? Inasmuch as this question of resource allocation has been nagging national politics since the creation of the United States, the politicized and inefficient budgeting process illustrates the risk of squander. The individual states share an interest in being more prepared, but they cannot easily agree upon exactly how it should be done, and while they debate, time is wasted and resources that could be put to use are idle instead. Indeed, there may well be no clear way to settle the problem of resource allocation in the face of an asymmetric threat potential. And in the meantime, while the allocation process appears to be

---

[38] Of course, national governments no less than insurance companies occupy themselves with the development of algorithms to model and estimate levels of risk. The US Department of Defense's Office of Net Assessment has received particular notoriety in this regard, in part due to the profile of its director, Andrew Marshall.

a necessary step toward preparedness, in fact available response capacity is being squandered *while the process is under way.*

As with blowback, squander is all too familiar among business organizations seeking to become more strategically prepared for change in the environment. One example of a company that squandered its resources in an attempt to become more prepared is *Berlingske*, one of the largest daily newspapers in Denmark, which in the mid 1990s faced the uncertainty of the emerging Internet.[39] To deal with this challenge, the CEO assembled a task force to determine what influence electronic media would have on its newspapers. The task force was responsible for recommending to the Board a 'new media' strategy for *Berlingske*, and three of its five members were also members of the company's management committee.

Soon this task force decided to create a second group of younger line managers from the different departments in the company, which served two purposes. First, to involve department staff in the strategy process and to keep them informed (both formally and informally) of electronic media and current trends in the industry. Second, to generate new ideas and act as a sounding board for the more senior task force. Anticipating a management decision based on the recommendations from the task force, during the next few months the company launched only modest initiatives involving electronic media.

During the next four months these groups worked in parallel and met occasionally. The junior group came to focus on planned or in-place electronic projects, analysing departmental strengths and weaknesses vis-à-vis electronic media and identifying new potential projects for their

---

[39] This story is adapted from 'The Berlingske Group: Looking at the Future of Electronic Media', by M. Schweinsberg, J.-H. Aadne, J. Roos, and G. von Krogh (1997) IMD Case Study, GM 656.

departments. The more senior group spent five out of seven meetings discussing the overall purpose of the newspaper, and if electronics versions of media were permissible given their purpose statement. At the junior group's final meeting four months later, members presented departmental recommendations for potential projects to the senior group. A member commented on the atmosphere in the group: 'When we presented our project recommendations, some people said things like, 'If *Berlingske* doesn't do this, then I'll do it myself. Most of us really see the importance of electronic media, here and now.'

When the senior group presented its findings (and those of the junior group) to the management committee and board, their presentation emphasized three facts: (i) their competition was moving fast to launch new initiatives; (ii) their qualified staff advocated the development of new projects as well as a clear mandate from the Board; and (iii) one of the company's largest advertising accounts had started its own home page, and printing homepage addresses of advertisers was becoming commonplace in newspapers. The presentation included a list of fifty potential electronic media projects with detailed cost estimates. Finally, the task force asked that the Board give a clear indication of what *Berlingske*'s level of ambition should be concerning electronic media. For the first time throughout the strategy practice, during that presentation the CEO took an official positive stance for electronic media. A senior executive said: 'It was good to have his support. Now we are waiting for the Board to come back to us.'

A few days after the task force presentation, and before the board had returned with a decision about how the organization should proceed, *Berlingske*'s main competitor *Jyllands-Posten* surprisingly presented itself to the world as the Danish 'Internet Newspaper'. However, not even this competitive move caused the *Berlingske* Board or the CEO to make the expected decisions during the weeks to come. In the meantime, *JyllandsPosten* flooded the market with their own, electronic-media based innovations, and *Berlingske* staff expressed extreme frustration about the time and resources that had been squandered on the formal strategy process.

6.4 Zones of 'acceptable' risk

In the preceding sections we have suggested that the tactical risks faced by organizational leaders who take strategic action in response to the need for preparedness include diminished returns, blowback and squander. We have not considered in any detail the factors that might contribute to, or detract from efforts to manage these risks. But whatever these factors may be, the practical problem remains as follows: the thinkable level of threat can drive the need for preparedness past the organization's capacity to overcome it. And as we have seen above, this problem becomes more difficult for organizational leaders to deal with because any action runs the tactical risk of making the problem worse.

It has been argued that this reflexive internalization of risk within the decision process is unique to our contemporary historical period (Beck, 1992). Whether or not this historical claim is true, it seems clear enough that as strategists and organizational leaders in the field of preparedness today reach the limits of what is thinkable and possible, they have no choice but to 'accept' a certain degree of risk (Figure 9) in order to operate at all.

The logic of Figure 9 is thus as follows:

- As the need for preparedness approaches the limits of the thinkable and the possible, organizational leaders can find themselves severely constrained by tactical risks that pertain to any course of strategic action; and

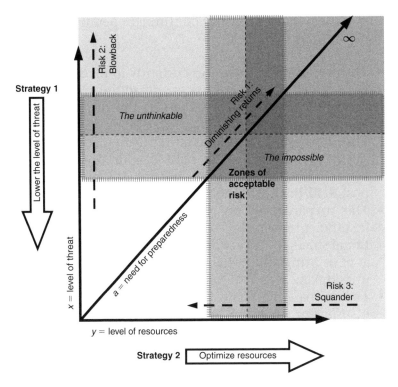

Figure 9   Zones of acceptable risk

- therefore, pending unforeseen future events, they must explicitly define 'zones of acceptable risk' within which the structure and operation of the organization can be managed and maintained.

The narrative illustrations we have considered thus far provide examples of organizations operating within these zones of acceptable risk, with both positive and negative results. In view of these case stories, and working with the logic that we have traced out from the CFR claim in the series of figures, we can identify a series of distinct claims that leaders make to justify continued operation within zones of acceptable risk:

- The preparedness measures currently in place are sufficient, given the level of risk, so no additional strategic action is necessary (for example, the pre-9/11 Bush administration position on al-Qaeda).
- The preparedness measures currently in place are insufficient given the level of risk, so additional strategic action is both necessary and possible (for example, the post-9/11 Bush administration position on al-Qaeda).
- The preparedness measures currently in place are insufficient given the level of risk, and although additional strategic actions are necessary and possible, these actions bring additional risks, and thus should not be undertaken.
- The preparedness measures currently in place are insufficient, given the level of risk, and although additional strategic actions are necessary, they are impossible given the existing resources and so should not be undertaken.
- The preparedness measures currently in place are insufficient, given the level of risk, and although additional, necessary strategic actions seem impossible and/or overwhelmingly risky, they must be attempted anyway in the name of some value greater than the organization itself.

In any case, where strategic decisions such as these are made, the 'acceptability' of risk remains subject to question, and frequently that questioning has moral and even legal dimensions. For example, in 1999, KPMG decided to offer a tax shelter service offering 'Blips' to companies and wealthy individuals. Blips enabled these clients to claim artificial losses worth a total of USD 4.4 billion on their tax returns, which could be offset against income and capital gains. Already in September 2000, the

IRS classified Blips as a potentially abusive tax shelter, and the service was discontinued. By that time, KPMG had pocketed no less than USD 53 million in fees from 186 clients.

As US authorities probed into how senior leaders in KPMG decided to launch the service, they lifted the lid on the role played not only by KPMG, but additionally by the other big accounting firms in the highly aggressive and very lucrative tax avoidance industry. By July 2005, the US Department of Justice was considering whether or not to bring criminal charges against KPMG, which according to *Financial Times* and other observers would 'make or break' the entire firm.[40] With memories of Anderson's Enron-induced collapse in 2002 in mind, some observers worried such charges would damage the entire industry by reducing to three the remaining global accounting firms. And in hindsight, the ex-CEO of KPMG told the *Financial Times* in April 2005 that he had 'a tremendous amount of personal regret about the whole matter.'

This admission illustrates how what may have seemed like an acceptable risk at the time becomes 'regrettable' down the road. Indeed, the legal parameters that KPMG and its competitors may (or may not) have crossed are themselves subject to change, driven by broader shifts in society and culture.

In this sense, while judgments about acceptable risk may draw on scientific data for support, they cannot ultimately be made exclusively on the basis of empirical evidence or rational hypothesis. Hard scientific data and data-gathering techniques are certainly required in order to assess the risk, but in order to make the decision that a particular risk is 'acceptable', leaders must additionally have recourse to *values*.

---

[40] Financial Times, 11 July 2005, 'Bathroom metaphors shed light on KPMG tax avoidance probe,' p. 17.

7.0
Making Value Judgments

When the increased need for preparedness comes as a surprise, strategists and organizational leaders must balance between decreasing the level of threat and increasing their resource utilization capacities. As they do, they have to deal with squander, blowback and diminishing returns as tactical risks.

But even in relatively mundane circumstances, as organizations strive to think the unthinkable, the future remains uncertain. And as organizations strive to extend their potential for strategic response, this potential means nothing unless it can be translated into effective action.

Thus from a strategic leadership perspective, preparedness in the face of an asymmetric threat potential involves not only the effective management of available resources or the effective mitigation of the resource need. Additionally, preparedness may involve the judgment that 'enough is enough' even in the face of overwhelming hypothetical need. Or conversely, preparedness may involve the judgment that it is better to expend all resources in the service of a non-economic or non-instrumental objective, for example, in the name of freedom, happiness, or some other ideological objective.

In order for an organization to balance within the zones of acceptable risk at the limits of knowledge and action, it is necessary therefore for its leaders to have recourse to something that cannot be known by any logical necessity nor proven by any empirical evidence. When strategists and leaders confront the practical problem of preparedness, they require not only the best available knowledge about the threat and the optimal resource utilization capacity. Additionally, they must have recourse to values that are grounded in intuition, belief, and affective sensitivity. In other words, leaders who effectively face the strategic challenge of preparedness must not only be knowledgeable and capable, but additionally, they must be *ethical*.

Of course, to the extent that economics even for Adam Smith could be understood as an applied sub-field of ethics, all organizational activity can be understood as implicitly or explicitly normative, for better or worse. But in modern, bureaucratic, and institutionally organized systems, leaders do not necessarily have to confront, or reflect on that normativity on a regular basis.[41]

The challenge of preparedness forces leaders, however, to articulate why an organization should attempt the impossible or, conversely, face the unthinkable. And while such arguments can be made in economic terms, ultimately they must be justified in reference to some value-based notion of a particular way of life that is worth sustaining. Even though the 'fog of war' can drive the social process of defining and advocating particular forms of well-being down the list of strategic priorities, individual decision-makers must recognize that when they court fate by deeming certain risks 'acceptable', they render

---

[41] We are particularly indebted on this point to insights contributed by Dr. Bart Victor, Cal Turner Professor of Moral Leadership Owen Graduate School of Management, Vanderdilt University in discussion.

themselves subject to the moral praise or blame of their organizational colleagues, fellow citizens and critics.[42]

In this sense, faced with the practical problem that arises when the need for preparedness stretches beyond the organization's available resources, leaders can certainly draw on the best available knowledge and the best available skills as they seek strategically to respond. But as the need for preparedness approaches the limits of what is thinkable or possible, they must additionally make normative, ethical judgments concerning the acceptability of risk. In this sense, we suggest that the need for preparedness calls for leadership that is involving the creative expression and enactment of ethical values.

In the interest of developing greater awareness and understanding about how our ethical values drive our intrinsically normative decisions about acceptable risks, we will in the following pages look at how the habit of striking ethical balances at the limits of knowledge and action has been described by philosophers, political scientists, lawyers, psychologists, and organizational scholars in terms of *practical wisdom.*

---

[42]A particularly poignant example of this situation can be found in Errol Morris' 2003 documentary film, *The Fog of War: Eleven Lessons from the Life of Robert S. McNamara.* Other examples include the 'perp walking' executives – once heros on plaques and pedestals, now goats in jail.

8.0

Re-framing the Strategic Response to Unexpected Change[43]

As we have seen, the strategic challenge of how organizations can become more prepared for unexpected events has risen significantly on the leadership agenda following the events of 9–11.[44] As we have also seen, strategists who 'think the unthinkable' increasingly confront a particular practical problem. In short, the various 'thinkable' scenarios can appear so great (in number as well as in scale) that the task of becoming adequately prepared for them all stretches the limits of available resources. This practical problem becomes acute when the resources required to build up a response capacity in anticipation of a series of 'thinkable' events exceeds the sum total of resources available. And in the most extreme case, the costs of preparedness

---

[43] Portions of the following sections have appeared previously as M. Statler and J. Roos (2006) 'Reframing Strategic Preparedness: An Essay on Practical Wisdom', *International Journal of Management Concepts and Philosophy*, 2 (2): 99–117.

[44] *Managing Risk: An Assessment of CEO Preparedness* (2004) provides an exemplary, practitioner-oriented account of this challenge, including data that compare the perceived threat of terrorist attack to the perceived threat of currency fluctuation, among other events (Price WaterhouseCoopers, 2004).

can exceed the total value of that organization which seeks preparedness in the first place.[45]

When the need for preparedness stretches beyond the organization's available resources, leaders require the best available knowledge and the best available skills as they seek to respond strategically. But additionally, as the need for preparedness approaches the apparent limits of what is thinkable or possible, strategists have no choice but to make normative, ethical judgments concerning the acceptability of certain risks. In this sense, the need for preparedness requires strategic leadership that is ethical, i.e., based on values.

We therefore attempt to re-frame the response to the challenge of preparedness in terms of *practical wisdom*.[46] This ancient ethical concept has been recently revived within the humanities and social sciences, and special attention has been paid to practical wisdom as a peak, or excellent form of human action that involves, but is distinct from rational knowledge (for example, Sternberg, 1998; Baltes and Kunzmann, 2004). Management and organizational scholars have explored the relevance of practical wisdom to strategizing under conditions of uncertainty (Wilson and Jarzabkowski, 2004), to ethical action in the face of unexpected change (Tsoukas and Cummings, 1997), and to the forms of management education that appear to contribute to the development of such capacities (Clegg and Ross-Smith, 2003). Our own consideration of the concept (Statler and Roos, 2006; Statler et al., 2006; Statler, 2005; Roos, 2006) is both informed by and addressed to the growing stream of literature that seeks to understand the 'practices' involved with strategy in organizations (see,

---

[45] The CFR report formulation echoes: 'We could spend our entire GNP and still be unprepared.' (2003).

[46] Cf. Aristotle (1962), and for a comprehensive reprise in modern philosophical terms, cf. Gadamer (2002 [1960]).

for example, Balogun, Huff and Johnson, 2003; Hendry and Seidl, 2003; Heracleous, 2003; Jarzabkowski, 2004; Johnson, Melin and Whittington, 2003; Régner, 2003; Whittington, 2002). Within this literature, it has been suggested that the concept of practical wisdom provides a way to describe a particular form of intelligence that is most appropriate for dealing effectively *and* ethically with unexpected change (Wilson and Jarzabkowski, 2004), but this suggestion has not yet been fully explored.

Thus in the interest of guiding future research focused on the specific practices that contribute to strategic preparedness, we here conduct a more detailed and thorough exploration of the concept of practical wisdom, its heritage, and its significance for management and organization studies.

We begin with a genealogy in which we explore the origins of the concept of practical wisdom in ancient Greek philosophy, as well as its modern vestiges in various academic disciplines (including philosophy and psychology, as well as organization studies). Then we continue with a presentation of an interpretative framework that includes elements of the existing 'balance theory' of wisdom (Sternberg, 1998), as well as extensions of that theory that we believe make it more amenable for use in organizational contexts. We then devote the rest of the book to an exploration of the significance of the concept of practical wisdom for researchers focused on the 'practice' of strategy, as well as for those strategists and leaders who are confronted by the challenge of preparedness.

9.0
A Genealogy of Practical Wisdom

9.1 Ancient roots

In order to understand what the term 'practical wisdom' refers to, we begin by considering a distinction drawn thousands of years ago between scientific knowledge, cunning intelligence, and practical wisdom. In the *Nicomachean Ethics*, Aristotle claims that scientific knowledge ('episteme') seeks to understand the necessary laws and principles of things in the natural world. Aristotle's articulation of this claim (in the *Ethics*, as well as the *Physics* and the *Metaphysics*) has provided a foundational touchstone for of all the modern traditions of inquiry in the natural sciences – where every appearance of change or transformation is generally presumed to occur in accordance with a principle or law which itself does not change, but holds by necessity and in eternity.

Distinct from science, according to Aristotle, is cunning intelligence ('metis'), which seeks not truth but advantage. In the *Nicomachean Ethics*, Aristotle associates this form of intelligence with military generals who seek victory, politicians who seek to convince other people using rhetoric, and doctors who seek to preserve health. Aristotle introduces these examples to illustrate contexts for action in which the means of action are not nearly so important as the end, which is sought for its own sake. This form of intelligence was certainly prized by the ancient Greeks – recall, for example, Odysseus, whose cunning enabled him to survive his great voyage and make it home in time to save his lonely wife from marauding suitors. At the same time, the Greeks also recognized that cunning could present significant dangers to the well-governed state, especially insofar as it could involve deception and lawlessness in pursuit of advantage.

Aristotle rejected the notion that scientific knowledge could be applied to the human social world because he assumed at an ontological level that it was too complex and unpredictable to be known with any certainty. At the same time, he did not believe that cunning alone was capable of promoting the 'good life' – indeed, he was generally skeptical about using the goals of an action to justify its means, and he flatly refused to accept the notion (later popularised by Machiavelli) that 'might makes right'. By extension, we can say that, on the one hand, Aristotle rejected the contemporary positivist search for formal, *a priori* content and process variables pertaining to strategic management, while on the other hand, he rejected the neoclassical economic theory that the pursuit of competitive advantage on an individual or collective basis was a moral good in itself.

Precisely in view of the tension between science and cunning, Aristotle helps us to define practical wisdom ('phronesis') as *the virtuous habit of making decisions and taking actions that serve the common good*. This distinct form of human intelligence effectively serves the good of the community even in the face of ambiguous or uncertain circumstances. Thus precisely where the predictive capacity of scientific knowledge breaks down, practical wisdom addresses normative considerations about what in future *should* occur. Similarly, though practical wisdom may draw on cunning to realize such normative goals, it disciplines cunning to avoid deception and to focus on advantages that may be shared by society.

In this sense, the term 'practical wisdom' refers to an optimal (that is, 'virtuous') orientation toward uncertainty and risk. The practically wise individual recognizes that actions are always constrained to some extent by fate, luck, and contextual circumstances – and yet precisely in view of such circumstances, acts in such a way as to preserve and enhance the well-being ('eudaimonia') of society.

If we parse Aristotle's conceptualization of practical wisdom more carefully,[47] we find that it includes four distinct elements that are directly relevant to the practical problem of preparedness that we identified above. First, where the need for preparedness begins with the question 'prepared for what scenario(s)?', practical wisdom involves first and foremost the (thinkable) goals and desires of the individual who seeks to make a judgment and take action. Secondly, where organizational leaders must define parameters of acceptable risk and justify actions taken (or not taken) at the limits of the thinkable and the possible, practical wisdom involves the affirmation that actions such as the one in question are good for the community of stakeholders. Third, where leaders and strategists select specific strategies and tactics in response to the need for preparedness, practical wisdom involves the explicit claim that, based on available information and perceptions, the specific action in question will provide an instantiation of that ethical value. And finally, because Aristotle would be unwilling to concede that anyone could truly know what is good for society without actually doing it, practical wisdom necessarily involves the habit of taking the action itself.

As we take Aristotle's conception of practical wisdom as a starting point for our own consideration of its

---

[47] In this passage we follow an analysis presented in MacIntyre (1981: 161–2).

relevance to the challenge of preparedness, it is important to acknowledge the extent to which this ancient tradition of interest in wisdom has faded significantly with the rise of modern sciences over the last several hundred years. Indeed, while for centuries wisdom flourished as a complement and guide to the sciences, following the Enlightenment it came to be associated more readily with theology and folktales, deemed a softer, second cousin to science, incapable of generating the kinds of fact-based, 'hard' truth necessary for modern life. Management as a form of reflective social practice has itself arisen within the modern, scientific prejudice toward necessity and against uncertainty, that is, toward knowledge of objective laws and principles, against subjective normativity. For better or for worse, this prejudice holds even more firmly within the academic tradition of management studies than it does among practicing managers.

Thus we acknowledge that by re-framing the strategic response to the challenge of preparedness in terms of practical wisdom, we risk losing the attention of those scholars and practitioners who have been trained to prefer the certainty of the empirical sciences (together with its formal models, statistical analyses, and so on) to the vagaries of politics and ethics. In deference to these colleagues and critics, we point out that of all contemporary human pursuits, management, precisely to the extent that it deals directly with the uncertainty, ambiguity, and unpredictability of the future, appears uniquely to stretch the limits of scientific understanding and to call for alternative epistemological frameworks.

To be sure, many scholars and proponents of 'scientific management' may regard the popular business section in the bookstore as a pile of claptrap equivalent in rigor and bottom-line value to the spirituality or self-help sections. Without denying the importance of methodological rigor and peer review for the human sciences, we regard the ongoing proliferation of practitioner-oriented management books simply as evidence that people continue in spite of the bias toward science to seek (precisely by reading the personal anecdotes offered by successful leaders, gurus and CEOs) what Aristotle and many others have referred to as practical wisdom.

Our pragmatic question is: to what extent can this latent practitioner-driven interest in wisdom be cultivated and refined in such a way as to have a positive impact for those organizations that struggle to become more prepared for the unexpected? We suggest that any attempt to answer this question should take into consideration the various research streams within different fields of study that currently focus on the relevance of practical wisdom for today's world.

9.2   Modern vestiges

If we follow the standard academic disciplinary segmentations, there is little doubt that the significance of 'practical wisdom' is discussed and debated most frequently and most intensely among philosophers. Aristotle's differentiation of ethics from physics and metaphysics was so decisive that it shaped and guided two thousand years' worth of philosophical writing and teaching – indeed today no professional ethicist worth his or her salt would dare be caught in the campus pub without an opinion or two about Aristotle's concept of *phronesis*. Within the canonical echo chamber of 'the Western philosophical tradition' such opinions are typically articulated in accordance with subsequent sub-streams of commentary, on Aristotle's notion, notably including the classical Stoics, the medieval Thomists, the German Romantics, the utilitarians, the virtue ethicists, and so on.

We should therefore acknowledge that there is a contemporary stream of interest in practical wisdom focused on moral values that are conservative in their political orientation.[48] There is also a strand of interest in practical wisdom focused on interpretative theories of political action and ethical obligation that take a much more liberal, hermeneutic viewpoint on justice in a participatory democracy.[49] For our purposes, this point of tension only further illustrates how at the limits of knowledge and action a need arises for value judgments. Whether the well-being of an individual or a community should be judged with respect to traditional, conservative values or instead with respect to progressive, liberal values – both cases support our claim that the need for preparedness calls for practical wisdom, not exclusively for science or cunning.

These outlines of the philosophical tradition provide rough indications of its breadth and depth, though it remains impossible to account for it comprehensively here. It may, however, be possible to identify that philosophical conceptualization of practical wisdom that seems most appropriate to the strategic challenge of preparedness as we have defined it.

In that respect, insofar as the need for preparedness stretches the limits of what is thinkable and possible, strategy researchers cannot rely on a conceptualization that begins with or leads to any kind of moral truth or certainty. Similarly, we must avoid any conceptualization that cleaves to any otherworldly or metaphysical principles. Finally, we must avoid any suggestion that practical wisdom refers to a codifiable quantum of information that can, as it were, be known independently of the unexpected event itself.

Instead, the need for preparedness points toward those philosophical conceptualizations of practical wisdom

---

[48]Here, see the influence of Leo Strauss on the neoconservative movement in government as well as on the streams of philosophical ethics that appeal implicitly or explicitly to conservative religious or theological principles.

[49]See, for example, the entire series of publications in Verso under the heading 'Phronesis', edited by Ernesto Laclau.

that emphasize processes of interpretation, focus concretely on the here-and-now, and refer to the performative enactment[50] of the common good. These criteria point particularly toward the conception of practical wisdom articulated by Hans-Georg Gadamer, who in his discussion of Aristotle's ethics claims that 'we do not learn moral knowledge, nor can we forget it. We do not stand over against it, as if it were something that we can acquire or not, as we can choose to acquire an objective skill ... Rather, we are always already in the situation of having to act ...' (Gadamer, 2002 [1960]: 317). On Gadamer's analysis, practical wisdom refers to the immanent and ongoing interpretive process of evaluating both means and ends, and applying schemata (that is, ideals, principles) that emerge only as they are concretized in and through the action itself. In this sense, we can say that in the face of an unexpected or ambiguous event, the common good is performatively enacted (in ways that Gadamer goes on to characterize as playful and creative) in and through a practically wise response.[51]

If Gadamer's conceptualization of practical wisdom seems to raise more questions than it answers, we may characterize that effect as intrinsic to philosophy, or we may equally affirm the pragmatic, even ethical relevance

---

[50] We use this term following Hodgkinson (2005).

[51] Again, we confront the difference between theoretical, epistemic understanding and practical or ethical understanding. We should note that the claim that ethics (not metaphysics) is the 'first philosophy' has been raised by Levinas. What Gadamer refers to as the ethical significance of philosophical method arises in an adjacent stream of political and social philosophical debate (including, for example, Habermas, Rawls and Sen) concerning justice. Gadamer himself claims that the social sciences cannot be distinguished from morality, and in this way sides with Foucault's claims that knowledge and power are inextricably linked.

of such an unsettling process.[52] But for better or for worse, the behavioral sciences are by contrast more directly conditioned by the drive to settle questions rather than raise them. And so we now turn to consider how psychologists have begun in the last few decades to work through the philosophical tradition and situate the concept of practical wisdom with respect to modern theories of intelligence.

Among psychologists, practical wisdom is now variously characterized as 'an expert knowledge system' (Baltes and Kunzmann, 2004), as 'the application of intelligence, creativity and knowledge' (Sternberg, 2004), and as 'an integration of cognitive, reflective and affective personality characteristics' (Ardelt, 2004: 274). Practical wisdom has also been associated with such positive human qualities as good judgment skills, psychological health, humor, autonomy, and maturity.[53] Educational psychologists have further emphasized the importance of imagination for the development and exercise of wisdom (Noel, 1999a).

But again, the peculiar constraints inherent in the organizational challenge of preparedness direct our attention toward one particular psychological conception of wisdom. According to the 'balance theory' (Sternberg, 1998; 2001; 2004), practical wisdom involves

> 'the application of intelligence, creativity, and knowledge to the common good by balancing intrapersonal (one's own), interpersonal (others'), and extrapersonal (institutional or other larger) interests over the long and short terms, through the mediation of values, so as

---

[52] As Anthony Kronman, Yale Law School dean calls (1995) for the return of the 'lawyer-statesman' capable of practically wise decisions and actions, he recognizes the importance of this questioning method (and its limits) for the practice of law.

[53] Citation information for each of these qualities can be found in Ardelt (2004: 280).

to adapt to, shape and select environments.' (Sternberg, 2004: 287)

We will address this theory in greater detail below – but for the moment we wish to underscore how the emphasis on balance (a direct inheritance from Aristotle) requires an integrated understanding of the relationships between the individual, the organization, and the world around them. Indeed, decisions and actions taken in the name of preparedness should not be understood as generic functions that exist independently of the context – instead, precisely because it addresses a future that cannot be known, preparedness remains necessarily context-specific, provisionally balancing on the threshold of uncertainty. In this sense, practical wisdom is not a body of knowledge, but instead an embodied habit, a performative act of 'playing the game'.[54]

Continuing our genealogy of practical wisdom in contemporary scholarship, we find that the relevance of such game-playing virtuosity has not been ignored by organizational scholars, who have also begun to focus increasingly on practical wisdom as a way to describe normatively optimal or 'virtuoso' performance in the face of uncertainty or ambiguity. Clegg and Ross Smith write, for example, that:

> Management is bounded by great depths of uncertainty and ignorance within which it is constituted, which is what makes the discipline a candidate for treatment as an example of 'phronesis' rather than of

---

[54] This notion of practical wisdom as a practice of play has been elaborated by Dreyfus and Dreyfus (1986), as argued in Flyvbjerg (2001) and Halverson (2004). Bourdieu also invokes play as a metaphor for the exercise of practical reason (1998), and this characterization must be considered in view of his broader theory of human social action, especially with regard to the concepts of 'habitus' (which he defines explicitly in reference to the Aristotelian notion of virtue as a '*hexis*') or habituated practice.

a context-independent, objective and value-free ratio-nalist science. Phronesis, an Aristotelian term, refers to a discipline that is pragmatic, variable, context depend-ing, based on practical rationality, leading not to a concern with generating formal covering law-like explanations but to building contextual, case-based knowledge. (Clegg and Ross-Smith, 2003: 86)

In turn, Tsoukas and Cummings acknowledge that the contextual, case-based knowledge typical of *phronesis* represents a much-needed departure from the tradition of 'scientific management':

> The formal-cum-abstract mode of reasoning which was so highly valued by the early organization theorists (see, e.g., Thompson, 1956: 103) is now seen as too crude to account for a multifaceted and ambiguous real-ity. Practical knowledge is no longer conceived in quasi-algorithmic terms, as the application of generic formulae, but in terms of acting wisely, being able to close the 'phronetic gap' (Taylor, 1993: 57) that almost inevitably exists between a formula and its enactment. (Tsoukas and Cummings, 1997)

Wilson and Jarzabkowski have tried to show how practi-cal wisdom becomes relevant whenever strategists exhaust the capacity of algorithms and formal models to guide the organization:

> Practical wisdom has much to do with the skill and knowledge of the strategist, who realizes both existing knowledge of the market and firm and its aspirations practically, through the performance of a particular strategy, involving multiple negotiations, truces, agree-ments, investments and commitments (Hendry, 2000). Practical wisdom thus captures the oscillation between animation and orientation that comprises strategic

thinking and acting (Cummings and Wilson, 2003). It is, however, an under-researched topic so that we lack a comprehensive understanding of what constitutes the political, social, cultural, conceptual and material resources through which such oscillation occurs. (Whittington, 2002). (Wilson and Jarzabkowski, 2004: 16)

The practice of psycho- and sociodrama emphasizes the emotional dimension of phronesis: *'our emotional reactions manifest, or indicate also the moral dimensions of the situation at hand'* (Roos, 2006: 215).[55] Hands-on, playful methods combined with (spontaneous) drama sometimes generate among strategists an emotional purging or cleansing similar to the catharsis[56] that originally was experienced by an ancient Greek audience at the end of a tragedy. The thoughts and emotions (positive and negative) released by thinking 'from within', during a state of spontaneity, are an integral part of phronesis and its cultivation:

> To make strategy practice more 'from within' means using all of our imagination and making way for the spontaneity of our wisdom. In my experience such profound transformation in thinking and doing does not happen by itself. We need to do it over, and over, and over again, and because of its emergent nature, when *Thinking From Within* we *should* expect a different outcome. (Roos, 2006: 236)

---

[55] Wisdom has been defined in the following way: *'We are wise when we act with split-second swiftness to cope with a surprising situation in a way that also benefits others'* (Roos, 2006: 216). For a review and definition of spontaneity as a heightened state of mind, see J. Roos and M. Roos, 'On Spontaneity' (2006), Working Paper 72, Imagination Lab Foundation, Switzerland (www.imagilab.org).

[56] The Greek word *katharsis* comes from *kathairein* (to purge) and from *katharos* (pure). For more of this see Roos (2006).

Reflecting back on the various ancient and modern streams of research in various fields traced in the preceding genealogy, we find a set of common considerations, including:

1 an interest in describing the form of human intelligence that is most relevant for, and most appropriate to, ambiguous or uncertain circumstances in which the limits of scientific knowledge and cunning action are approached or surpassed;
2 an acknowledgement that this unique form of intelligence must be both effective *and* ethical;
3 an acknowledgement that this form of knowledge includes emotion, embodiment, and social situatedness, as well as rational cognition; and
4 an emphasis on the extent to which this particular form of knowledge is associated with the creative enactment of the common good, or at least, with the intrinsic normativity of action.

We believe that these considerations have several provisional implications for how the strategic challenge of preparedness should be framed by theorists and practitioners of strategic management. First, as a concept, practical wisdom provides a meaningful way to describe the positive, 'best case' response to the need for preparedness. Secondly, as a virtuous pattern of behavior, practical wisdom can contribute to the preparedness objective at all organizational levels and on an ongoing basis. Finally, as a call to enact the common good, practical wisdom encourages strategists to deliberate carefully as they define parameters of 'acceptable risk'.

In an effort to explore these implications and discover how practical wisdom might emerge in specific organizational contexts, we now proceed with the development of our own dynamic model of practical wisdom.

10.0
An Interpretative Framework

Following the above genealogy, a number of crucial questions remain unanswered. Indeed, what is the common good? How is it defined? What evidence testifies to its presence or absence? How exactly is the relationship between certain habits of action and the common good to be determined?

As we have already indicated, entire traditions of debate within philosophy, as well as political science and economics, circle around such questions. Our endeavor in this book is not to settle these debates. Instead, we leave such questions concerning the common good to be answered by organizational actors themselves, while we focus our attention on developing an interpretative framework that allows management and organizational researchers to identify those practically wise activities that contribute to increased preparedness in organizations.

The framework that we develop does not necessarily imply direct, causal relations, but instead points toward potential nonlinear interactions between and among a multiplicity of factors. In this sense, it will hopefully guide future research that seeks to describe specific practices that are indicative of practical wisdom and its role with respect to the need for preparedness in organizational contexts.

10.1 The balance theory

From among the many different conceptualizations of practical wisdom cited above, we choose to base our interpretative framework on Robert Sternberg's balance theory of wisdom (Figure 10) for two reasons.

First, as we have already acknowledged, we find that the explicit emphasis on balance is most coherent with the Aristotelian differentiation between scientific knowledge and practical wisdom, and thus most appropriate to those situations in which the limits of the thinkable and the possible are approached. Second, with respect to the rhetoric as well as the logic of Sternberg's argumentation, we find the balance theory to be the most easily transportable across the boundaries of different fields, and the most amenable to theory development, given the methodological conventions particular to the field of organizational studies.[57]

Alongside these characteristics of the balance theory of practical wisdom which recommend it as a basis for our own interpretative framework, we also recognize several limitations or weaknesses. First, its cognitivist assumptions make it difficult to account for, much less to integrate, the perceptual, aesthetic, and affective dimensions of

---

[57] Whereas Gadamer's philosophical conception, for example, requires considerably more exegesis in order to present it in such a way as to be meaningful to management scholars and practitioners. While we hope one day to undertake this task, now is not the time for it. In any case, the question of 'theory development' presupposes an epistemology of empirical testing, and so on. Such assumptions may be slightly out of joint with the pragmatic epistemology that emerges 'from within' practical wisdom, where the endeavor to generate predictive hypotheses has already been rejected. Still, we are inspired by Sternberg's own 'scientific' efforts in this regard, and we believe that organizational theorists might pursue a similar path. Indeed, here Flyvbjerg (2001) shows the way with his articulation of the precepts guiding 'phronetic social science'.

human experience. And second, the dynamisms inherent in 'balance' are not adequately represented by the model – in other words, the processual aspects of practical wisdom are not acknowledged explicitly.[58] Although we

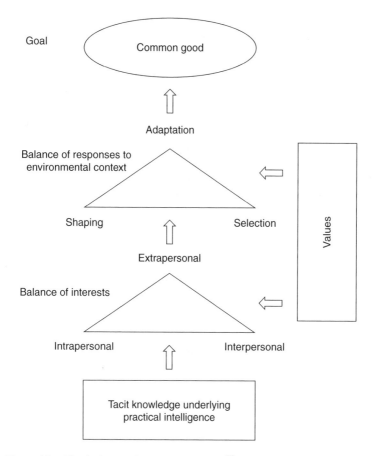

Figure 10   The balance theory of wisdom[59]

---

[58] Whereas within scientific rationality, time is the neutral dimension in accordance with which change can be independently measured, for practical wisdom time is experienced asymmetrically, and it involves history and memory, as well as desire and anticipation.
[59] From Sternberg (1998: 354).

will unfold these objections in more detail below, we believe that the balance theory remains coherent with the requirements articulated above.

As we have already seen, practical wisdom should not be considered as a quantity of information, nor as a functioning capacity that exists independently of the function it performs. Instead, practical wisdom refers to an habituated pattern of actions that are normatively positive both in terms of their process and in terms of their outcome. The balance theory addresses the habituated aspects of practical wisdom in terms of 'tacit knowledge'.[60] Furthermore, the balance theory indicates that every expression of our tacit knowledge is mediated through our values,[61] and thereby it captures the ethical normativity identified above. Finally, the balance theory uses the term 'common good' to describe the ethically normative goal or outcome of practically wise action.

Sternberg's model additionally indicates that any action based on tacit knowledge and mediated by values in such a way as to serve the common good involves two distinct balances: of interests, and of responses to the environment. The first of these balances pertains to intra-, inter- and extra-personal interests. Sternberg writes:

> What kinds of considerations might be included under each of the three kinds of interests? Intrapersonal interests might include the desire to enhance one's popularity or prestige, to make more money, to learn more, to increase one's spiritual well-being, to increase one's power, and so forth. Interpersonal interests might be

---

[60] Sternberg cites Polanyi (1976) as the source for his understanding of tacit knowledge.
[61] Sternberg cites Kohlberg (1969, 1983) as the source for his understanding of moral values, and by extension, of the common good as the highest of moral values.

quite similar, except as they apply to other people rather than oneself. Extrapersonal interests might include contributing to the welfare of one's school, helping one's community, contributing to the well-being of one's country, serving God and so forth. (Sternberg, 2001: 231)

In view of this variety of different interpretative possibilities, we suggest that the boundaries between the three distinct types of interest may be effectively traced in organizational preparedness discourses by paying attention to how subject pronouns (that is, the 'me', the 'us', and the 'them') are used. A plurality of distinct interests might in turn be effectively traced in organizations using stakeholder analysis methodologies, or even in reference to concepts of organizational identity.[62]

The second balance involves three distinct forms of response to the external environment. On this point Sternberg writes:

In adaptation, the individual tries to find ways to conform to the existing environment that forms his or her context. Sometimes adaptation is the best course of action under a given set of circumstances. But typically one seeks a balance between adaptation and shaping, realizing that fit to an environment requires not only changing oneself, but changing the environment as well. When an individual finds it impossible or at least implausible to attain such a fit, he or she may decide to select a new environment altogether, leaving, for

---

[62] Cf. Oliver and Roos (2005) and Roos (2006). For an account of how the broad, socio-cultural scope of this balance is performatively enacted in narrative and other forms of expression, cf. Benedict Anderson's *Imagined Communities: Reflections on the Origin and Spread of Nationalism*. Revised Ed. New York: Verso (1991).

example , a job, a community, a marriage, or whatever.
(Sternberg, 2001: 231)

We consider this balance of responses to the environment
as an acknowledgement both of the capacity of humans
to adapt to new circumstances, and of the limitations of
that capacity. More importantly, we suggest that although
the behaviorist logic of stimulus–response may adequately
describe the adaptation of certain natural phenomena,
the creative endeavor to shape existing environments and
select new ones involves a reflective capacity that cannot
easily be accounted for by classical behaviorist theories.
Instead, we suggest that the theoretical framework most
appropriate for future research on this balance is provided by the stream of complex adaptive systems theory
that emphasizes the autopoesis of human knowledge and
behavior (cf. von Krogh and Roos, 1995; Oliver and Roos,
2000), especially from a phenomenological perspective
(cf. Gallagher and Varela, 2001).

10.2   A dynamic model

In accordance with the shift from a static to a dynamic
ontology within strategic management outlined above
we believe that Sternberg's theory, however robust it may
be, requires additional elements before it can be considered appropriate for the strategic challenge of preparedness. As noted above, our basic objections are (i) that the
balance theory does not adequately account for the perceptual and other embodied dimensions of experience,
and (ii) that it does not adequately express the dynamisms
that are inherent in the balances.

We believe that the individual-level balances, as well as
the tacit knowledge, the values, and the notion of the common good remain in a more-or-less constant, dynamic
relationship to the social and material world, and that
these relationships are themselves historically-situated

and bound both by contingency and necessity with respect to an unpredictable future.[63] More specifically, we suggest that the mode of intentionality, the medium of action and the milieu in which actions take place remain crucially important for the description of practical wisdom in organizational contexts characterized by a need for preparedness.

First, where Sternberg claims that the balance of interests is struck in view of short- and long-term future, we suggest that the practice of dealing with short-, medium-, and long-term time horizons is a distinct balance unto itself. In colloquial terms, we could characterize these horizons in terms of 'now', 'soon', and 'later on' – but

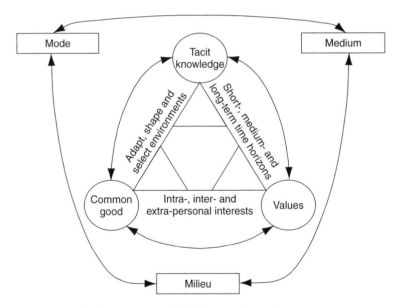

Figure 11   The dynamic model of practical wisdom

[63] On this point, and throughout the following section, we are indebted to Dr Greg Holliday, Director of the Assessment and Consultation Clinic at the University of Missouri-Columbia for his discussion inputs.

doubtless these terms could be rendered more precisely through a phenomenological analysis of time consciousness (cf. Heidegger, 1982, 1962). In any case, by distinguishing this third balance, we are able to emphasize the historically contingent duration of different responses to the environment (in addition to the duration of different interests).

Second, we transform the structural model of wisdom as a goal-oriented linear movement (that is, from tacit knowledge, mediated through values, and toward the common good), into a cyclical process in which each of these various dimensions of experience are co-constitutive of each other on an ongoing basis. It may seem at first like a category confusion to claim that the common good could have any indirect impact on the embodied tacit knowledge that people develop through experience. And yet, as Gadamer has argued, schemata such as the common good emerge and take shape only in and through the concrete circumstances for action. And values are performatively enacted whenever a practical judgment or appraisal of an uncertain situation is made. In this sense, we suggest that Sternberg's balance theory of wisdom can be extended if the common good, mediating values, and tacit knowledge are presented in such a way as to emphasize their interdependency or co-constitutive relation.

Third, we introduce three dynamisms pertaining specifically to the mode, medium, and milieu of practically wise action. We believe that these dynamisms mediate the three balances by shaping the emerging circumstances (both in the individual and in the environment) in which practical wisdom is expressed.[64] In this regard, we begin

---

[64]Again, complex adaptive systems theory may provide the most appropriate metaphors to describe the interaction between the balances and the dynamisms.

by suggesting that the degree of control or influence which can be exercised by any individual or any organization can be characterized in terms of a particular '*mode*' of intentionality.[65] Within the philosophical tradition, the term 'intentionality' is used technically to refer to the way in which mind or consciousness is always directed toward objects – epistemologically speaking, the possibility of meaning as such is grounded in 'intentionality'. Non-technical uses of the term typically focus on the deliberate, willful or volitional character of certain actions,

---

[65]As we turn then to problematize the mode of embodied intentionality we are inspired by Heidegger's differentiation between authentic and inauthentic 'modes' of intentional awareness. But rather than going at least initially or explicitly for the normative term 'authenticity', it seems more appropriate to stick with the purely logical modality and refer to the relative degree of possibility and/or necessity that characterizes the dynamic relations between beings. We could here follow out these dynamics as they function between the researcher and researched, as well as between the strategist or organization and its environment.

With respect then to different logical modalities, we can say that instrumental rationality privileges calculation and analysis to determine or approximate *necessary* relations (that is, principles, laws, causal necessity). Here, the neo-classical economic tradition provides a basis, and really any formal model within strategic decision making (for example, 5-forces, balanced scorecard, and so on) provides an instantiation or application of form of intentional awareness that privileges *necessary* relationships.

By contrast, practical wisdom would involve experimentation and action as a way to enact the possible. Here the model that most directly contrasts with *homo economicus* is *homo ludens*. There are several existing streams of strategy research that characterize strategy practice as a kind of creative enactment. For example, there is a stream of research that casts planning processes in terms of scenario learning (van der Heijden et al., 2002). In the context of strategy making we have identified serious play with the creative enactment of adaptive potential (Roos et al., 2004).

for example, 'I intentionally walked up the street and unintentionally bumped into a friend'.

By differentiating between distinct 'modes' of intentionality with respect to practical wisdom, we wish to emphasize that the relationships between tacit knowledge, values, and the common good are subject to dynamic change, depending on the circumstances. We submit that people can be more or less deliberate about, and indeed, differently aware of the balances that they are striking, or not. Moreover these different modes of intentionality are themselves not necessarily a matter of choice, but remain subject to dynamic change, both in the affective state of the individual and in the material and social context. In this sense, we suggest that the balance theory of wisdom can be fruitfully extended with the addition of 'mode' as another category of relevant empirical and experiential data.[66]

We also suggest that any attempt to balance interests, time horizons, and environments depends significantly on the *medium* through which actions and decisions are expressed. We can start in a very banal way to illustrate what we mean in reference to certain widespread, empirical patterns of activity. Traditionally, strategy work involves some amalgam of the following media: PowerPoint, spreadsheets, flip charts, emails, binders, verbal discussions, phone calls, and so on.[67]

---

[66] In this regard cf. the useful distinction drawn between deliberate and emergent strategy-making (Mintzberg and Waters, 1985).

[67] The significance of the medium for the embodied habit of practical wisdom has been addressed by recent organizational aesthetic theory in terms of its context-specific capacity to transmit 'schwung' energy, defined as a sensitive, aesthetic balance involving 'the pendulum movement between form and substance' (Guillet de Monthoux, 2004: 20).

While we are not quite willing to accept the proposition that 'the medium is the message', we are similarly unwilling to accept the pure, cognitivist assertion that propositional content, that is, meaning, exists completely independent of the form in which it is expressed. Stated positively, we believe that practical wisdom remains subject to dynamic change, depending on the media available for action and expression.[68] Moreover, this dynamism pertains not only to the action of the individual who would be considered practically wise, but also to the actions and expressions of other people which bear upon that individual.[69] In this sense, we suggest that the balance theory of wisdom can be fruitfully extended with the addition of 'medium' as another category of relevant empirical and experiential data.

Finally, we suggest that the values as well as the common good remain subject to all the dynamics within a given *milieu*. As above, we believe that any action that balances interests, time horizons, and environments, precisely to the extent that it draws on tacit knowledge, appeals to values, and enacts the common good, must be considered and deliberated about in view of its contextual circumstances. We use the term 'milieu' as it has been deployed generically within the social sciences to refer to the cultural, historical, and material context for human action. Additionally, to the extent that practically wise action must be considered 'appropriate' with respect to the context within which it emerges, we believe that the milieu can also be considered in aesthetic terms, where

---

[68] Although we fully acknowledge the importance of emotions in phronesis (cf. Roos, 2006), we will not elaborate this point in depth here.

[69] Indeed, from an actor-network theory perspective, we must equally consider the agency of non-human actors such as technological artifacts, bureaucratic structures, and so on.

judgments of beauty and proportion or 'fit' are relevant.[70] Our suggestion is simply that these various elements of the milieu stand in a dynamic relationship to what people consider practically wise. In this sense, we suggest that the balance theory of wisdom can be fruitfully extended with the addition of 'milieu' as another category of relevant empirical and experiential data.

On the whole, we believe that these three dynamisms extend the explanatory power of the balance theory of wisdom (i) by emphasizing the contextual factors that contribute to the fragility or the robustness of the balances, and (ii) by emphasizing the extent to which wisdom itself remains, in spite of every effort to develop it as a habit, subject to dynamic change.

In this sense, practical wisdom should not be misunderstood as an object that exists in the world, or as an objectively-identifiable personality trait that is possessed definitively by certain individuals and not by others. Instead, practical wisdom should be understood as a habit, a practice, a pattern of actions that can emerge in certain circumstances, just as it can fade in others. Furthermore, the attempt to describe and deliberate about whether or not a particular action exemplifies 'wisdom', should be understood as interpretative processes through which specific norms are created, perpetuated, altered, and disrupted.

---

[70] This connection between ethics and aesthetics was, of course, quite familiar to Aristotle. The modern tradition of dealing with this connection with respect to practical wisdom begins with Kant's insistence, in the *Critique of Judgment*, that the idea of common sense exemplified the experience of the beautiful. Pierre Guillet de Monthoux has recently dealt with this conceptualization at length and developed a series of interpretative models that emphasize the relevance of aesthetics for organizational life (cf. Guillet de Monthoux, 2004; Statler and Guillet de Monthoux, forthcoming).

We present this 'dynamic model of practical wisdom' as an interpretative framework that can (i) *help researchers as well as practitioners to reflect on the ethical dimensions of leadership and strategy practice in the preparedness field,* and thereby (ii) *encourage the development of habits that creatively enact the common good at the limits of the thinkable and the possible.*

11.0
Reflecting on the Model: Implications

In view of the practical problem confronting organizational leaders who find the need for preparedness stretching the limits of the thinkable and the possible, the preceding discussion has introduced the concept of practical wisdom and applied it to the challenge of preparedness in organizations. The implications are as follows.

First, practically wise habits appear to serve as means toward the end of preparedness to the extent that they can help to expand and extend what is thinkable and possible for the organization. By successfully balancing time horizons, interests, and relationships to the environment, strategy makers can gain new understanding, and by cultivating tacit knowledge they can extend the reach of action. And while such 'extensions' may remain unique to certain contextual or historical circumstances, we believe that it is nevertheless possible to describe and deliberate about practical wisdom in the actions of others. This activity can enable the creation of new ideas and new possibilities for action in present and future situations.

Second, given the ethical considerations that arise whenever certain parameters of risk are deemed 'acceptable', practical wisdom appears to provide organizational leaders and strategists with a normative ideal for action. Indeed, practically wise habits involve a qualitative improvement of human well-being on an everyday basis irrespective of the uncertainty of the future. With respect to preparedness in organizations, we believe that the promise of such improvement is best formulated as a series of critical questions. As organizations seek preparedness, what form of life are they affirming? How are the people in the organization thriving? How does that thriving impact on the thriving of others? By reflecting on such ethical questions at the limits of what is thinkable and what is possible strategists and organizational leaders can develop practically wise habits.

Of course, the practical problem confronting strategists and organizational leaders who respond to the need for preparedness will not go away just because they may exhibit practical wisdom. And ultimately, practical wisdom does not provide any predictive certainty about whether an organization is more or less prepared. What is worse, even when specific decisions and actions appear to exemplify practical wisdom, good ideas can still fail for unexpected reasons, while well-intended bad ideas can still lead to terrible consequences (as outlined above, including diminishing returns, blowback, and squander). And yet, precisely in view of these constraints, we suggest that practical wisdom provides a model of the form of human intelligence that is most suited to dealing ethically *and* effectively with such uncertainty, unpredictability, and risk.

The dynamic model of practical wisdom provides a way to describe how the definitions of 'acceptable risk', as well as the specific strategy practices involving 'acceptable risk', normatively balance time horizons, interests, and responses to the environment. For leaders and strategists, explicit awareness of these three balances can help to sharpen the definition of certain zones of acceptable risk. And in cases where organizations are surprised by the unthinkable and constrained by the impossible, the dynamic model of practical wisdom can help us to describe and deliberate about the extent to which specific practices enhance preparedness by enacting the common good.

We suggest that these implications are particularly relevant to the research stream focused on the practices involved with strategy. First, due perhaps to the dominance of scientific knowledge in the tradition of management research, the field retains a certain bias toward cognition and away from affect and aesthetics as categories of phenomena relevant to strategy practice. In this regard, we suggest simply that future strategy-as-practice research should be careful to integrate these and other important dimensions of embodied human experience alongside the cognitive and behavioral aspects of practice (For example, Merleau-Ponty, 1962; Varela et al., 1992).

Second, the prejudice for command-and-control notions of leadership and strategy practice is also deeply rooted in the history of management theory and practice. While we do not deny that this notion of intentionality may be effective (and even wise) under certain circumstances, its limits are reached when the formal structure of command is itself overwhelmed by an unexpected change. In such cases, not only are decentralized organizational decision-making structures required, but additionally, other modes of intentionality are required. Once the limits of thought and action have been surpassed, individuals may very well have no choice but to 'go with the flow' and see what emerges. In this respect, future research should focus on those practices through which emergent forms of intentional action are cultivated and encouraged (For example, Roos et al., 2004; Jacobs and Statler, 2005; Roos, 2006).

Finally, if we reflect critically on the practical problem that confronts strategists at the limits of the thinkable and the possible, one underlying reason why the threat potential appears overwhelming is that it presupposes a relatively passive, stimulus–response logic. But the challenge of preparedness need not involve scripted responses (and resource deployments) for each 'thinkable' scenario.[71] The concept of practical wisdom indicates that preparedness need not be considered in such strict, stimulus–response terms. Instead, preparedness-related practices could be cast proactively in terms of social construction and enactment. More specifically, preparedness could involve the creative enactment of the common good – and in a utopian, best-case scenario, the realization of shared well-being would simultaneously diminish the level of threat and extend the capacity for possible responses in an organization. We suggest that additional research in this area should therefore presuppose a fluid integration of decisions and actions within a specific historical and cultural milieu, while embracing and emphasizing the creative potential inherent in all human action.

---

[71] Specifically, with respect to the issue of responsiveness, we gesture toward the work of the German phenomenologist Bernard Waldenfels that differentiates response logics from the purely behaviorist, autistic response to the vigilant answer that is invented in the process of answering.

12.0
Developing Practically Wise Habits

In the interpretative framework presented above, practical wisdom refers to the virtuous habit of making decisions and taking actions that serve the common good. Accordingly, where the need for preparedness in organizations stretches beyond the limits of knowledge and action, practically wise individuals can deal with uncertainty in ways that are both ethical and effective. The question then becomes: *how* can people in organizations develop the practically wise habit of creatively enacting the common good?

We should emphasize at this point that for organizations facing the strategic problem of preparedness the relevance of practical wisdom depends crucially on the fact that it can be developed only as a *habit*. Practical wisdom is not an object or an information system that can be purchased and implemented in the organization, nor is it a source of knowledge or set of skills that can be outsourced to consultants or recruited and retained indefinitely as a human resource. It furthermore cannot be regulated from a governance perspective by a set of standards or enforced through industry compliance mechanisms. Of course, it may appear practically wise under certain circumstances for organizational leaders to take such measures in the name of preparedness, but the metrics and measures should be understood as exhaustible means to other ends (for example, threat mitigation, resource optimization), and should therefore not be confused with the practical wisdom required to judge the appropriateness of the means/ends relationship itself.

As we have seen already, practical wisdom involves a habit of striking a series of balances (that is, of time, interests and environments). We have seen how the 'common good' is creatively enacted as these balances are struck by individuals *in situ*. The balances and the common good that they enact are therefore not ahistorical or temporally discreet but instead rooted in experience and bound by individual memory and cultural history. As such, they cannot be taught by the traditional means of classroom instruction, where expert knowledge and information is communicated uni-directionally *from* an instructor *to* a group of students. Instead, the form of education that cultivates practical wisdom must involve all the richness of human experience, that is, the entire body with all of its senses rather than just the mind. And as we will see in the following pages, the cultivation of practical wisdom also requires reflection on that experience, deliberation about it, and re-engagement in practice.

These unique constraints may make the endeavor to develop practical wisdom in organizations seem like an outright waste of time – indeed, cynical organizational leaders and strategists might object that, as with genius or charisma, you either have practical wisdom or you don't, and in any case, such habits need to be hired rather than developed. We acknowledge this objection, especially as it may arise from within a milieu where the need for preparedness appears so pressing as to make any longer-term personal or organizational development agenda appear foolish. And yet, we have already shown (cf. 7.0 Value Judgements, p. 65) that it is precisely this potentially infinite need for preparedness which calls for values-based decisions and actions. In deference to this objection, even as we insist that the development of practical wisdom in organizations requires longer-term habituation through experience, we focus on how it might be developed on an ongoing basis, precisely in and through the practices of everyday organizational life.

The extreme case illustration of the 9–11 attacks in New York and Washington, DC can be considered as an excellent opportunity to develop practical wisdom through experience. Indeed, because such opportunities come at great cost, the contemporary disaster-preparedness field has itself emerged to a certain extent as a collective attempt to learn from the 9–11 experience without actually having to go through it (again). At the same time, given the extent to which uncertainty and complexity affects organizational life on all levels on an everyday basis, it seems that such opportunities may exist at different levels of scale all around us, even though they remain difficult to seize.

In this light, we direct our attention toward those experiences that simulate the conditions of the need for preparedness without directly exposing organizations to the threat in question. In keeping with the logic of the CFR claim, as well as our interpretative model of practical wisdom, we now consider those practices or activities that *simulate* the following experiences:

- a confrontation with the limits of what is thinkable and possible;
- an occasion to experiment with, and reflect on the balances of interests, time horizons, and environments;
- exposure to (and thus, variation of) the mode, medium, and milieu dynamisms.

In the following pages, we will begin our consideration of such practices by describing what the Center for

Catastrophe Preparedness and Response (CCPR) at New York University (NYU) did during the early stages of its existence to develop preparedness as an organization, as well as for other organizations in the field. We then continue by reflecting on these findings in view of our theoretical and empirical research exploring the development of practical wisdom in and through strategy processes. Finally we will consider several recent proposals on how to advance management education. Throughout these sections, our purpose is to respond to the question about *how* people in organizations can develop the practically wise habit of creatively enacting the common good.

13.0

On the Front Lines: the Center for Catastrophe Preparedness and Response (CCPR) at New York University (NYU)[72]

As the federal government began in the months following the 9–11 attacks to allocate funds for catastrophe preparedness research and program development, New York University's Office of Federal Grants obtained a congressional allocation to fund a project that was envisioned as:

> one center in a critical location that could work closely with New York City and State, as well as the federal government, to look beyond the terrorist attacks and advise on how to best prepare for such future emergencies, catastrophes and disasters. (NYU Press Release, 2002)

This organization, the Center for Catastrophe Preparedness and Response (CCPR) at New York University (NYU), came into being in 2002 under the leadership of an interim director. By the summer of 2003 the organization began to hire a full-time, professional staff and directly to address

---

[72] Portions of the following sections have appeared previously as M. Statler, J. Roos and B. Victor (2006), 'Illustrating the Need for Practical Wisdom', *International Journal of Management Concepts and Philosophy*, 2 (1): 1–30. As noted previously, Matt Statler joined InterCEP, a program sponsored by CCPR, in January 2006 after this manuscript was completed.

the tasks set forth in its charter. At that time, we initiated contact with CCPR and began to gather data on its activities, culminating in a case study that we made available to the public in late 2003.[73] While CCPR's activities have evolved since that time in ways that merit further research, we focus our considerations in this chapter on the activities engaged in by CCPR staff during that initial time period of the second half of 2003.

At that time, we found that CCPR was struggling with a series of ambiguities pertaining to the definition of the catastrophic event itself, to the boundaries of the community affected by it (and furthermore, obliged to prepare for it), and to various tactical and strategic courses of action that would be required for preparedness, depending on the definitions of the problem and the community in question.

In keeping with the logic of the Council on Foreign Relations claim analysed above, we could now say that CCPR was struggling to think the unthinkable and to determine the limits of the possible, while at the same time struggling to determine how to frame the balance of interests for itself and for the preparedness field. So, then, as CCPR staff worked closely with local, state and federal officials at the front lines of the 9–11 events to resolve these struggles, what were they doing?

Over the course of an iterative process of data-gathering, reflection, and discussion with CCPR staff, we identified three patterns of activity that relate to the development of practically wise habits: (i) storytelling, (ii) dialogue with diverse groups of people, and (iii) integrated experience. We will now present an account of each of these three forms of activity, followed by a series of reflections on the relevance of these activities to the development of practical wisdom.

---

[73] That working paper was subsequently revised and published as cited in the previous footnote.

13.1   Storytelling: 'A million casualties'

In the course of their daily activities, CCPR staff spent a considerable amount of time engaged in the telling and sharing of stories with the various people with whom they were in contact. While the settings within which these stories were shared varied widely (from industry conferences, to academic conferences and presentations, meetings, phone calls, and so on), they typically involved a presentation either of direct personal experience in response to the 9–11 events, or of indirect experience based on the personal testimony of others.

Just as typically, the rhetorical gesture of presenting and reflecting on the story resembled that of a parable, where the contextual circumstances were set forth, a particular set of decisions or actions was described, the effects or implications of those decisions and actions were evaluated, and conclusions were drawn concerning how to become more prepared in the future.

Within this overall pattern of storytelling activity, in a deliberate effort to create a conversational frame within which they could effectively elicit potential funding needs from various organizations, CCPR began in late 2003 to tell a hypothetical story about 'one million casualties'. Referring to this story as 'Project LASER', CCPR explicitly stretched the limits of what was thinkable by dramatically increasing the scale of the impact of the catastrophic event. They used this narrative scenario as a way to identify the limits of what was possible for emergency and first-responder organizations. Faced with an asymmetric threat potential, this practice of imaginative storytelling allowed CCPR to stretch the limits of the thinkable in order to assess the current limits of the possible.

From a strategy-as-practice perspective, we believe that the activity of telling stories played a significant role in CCPR's attempts to learn from past experiences and identify opportunities to become more strategically prepared for similarly catastrophic events in the future.

13.2   Dialogue with diverse groups

At the same time, CCPR staff engaged in a related, though distinct pattern of activity involving dialogue with diverse groups of people. Working on the explicit assumption that 'there is potential in every sector of society' to contribute to achieving the objective of preparedness, CCPR sought from the beginning to position itself as relevant to every segment of the NYU community.[74] Beyond the NYU community, CCPR assembled an advisory board that includes members of city, state, and national government, as well as influential individuals in the private sector.[75] And beyond this group of advisors, CCPR engaged during late 2003 in dialogue with literally hundreds of individuals from dozens of organizations, gaining input from everyone from academics and policy-makers to firefighters and video game designers.

---

[74] This endeavor was exemplified by a meeting held in November, 2003 in which the deans from various NYU schools (including the Law School, Wagner School of Public Service, Medical School, School of Education, Arts and Sciences, and so on) were gathered so that CCPR staff could 'ring the bell as loud as we can ring it, basically tell them how we are organizing here and start discussing initiatives which they might have.'

[75] In particular, as of late 2003, this list included the Commissioner of the New York City (NYC) Police Department; the Senior Advisor for Counterterrorism to the Governor of New York State (NYS); the Director of Disaster Preparedness and Response from the NYS Governor's Office; the Director of the NYS Office of Public Safety, a national transportation expert from Parsons Brinkenhoff, the Commissioner of the NYC Office of Emergency Management, the Commissioner of the NYC Fire Department, an executive from the Greater New York Health Association, and the Chief Security Officer from Goldman Sachs.

For example, CCPR developed one project that brought together the diverse disciplines of computer science, law, and ethics. That project's conceptual framework held that the values of democratic, civil society can be embedded even in the design of technologies. The project was therefore based on the cross-disciplinary notion that technology design can actually play a major role in the capacity of independent, autonomous actors to organize and act, both in general and in the specific forms of collective action that are appropriate in the event of a catastrophe.

In view of many examples such as this one, we suggest that the practice of engaging in dialogue with diverse groups of people played a significant role in CCPR's attempts to learn from past experiences and identify opportunities to become more strategically prepared for similarly catastrophic events in the future.

13.3   Integrated experience

A third pattern of activity in which CCPR staff were engaged during late 2003 involved the exploration and development of technologies and processes designed to provide people in the preparedness field with training experiences that integrate as many aspects of the projected catastrophe experience as possible. In this sense, while CCPR affirmed the importance of storytelling and dialogue with diverse groups of people, they also recognized the importance of developing an embodied awareness of the many variables that might be expected to change dramatically in the event of a catastrophe.

At one level of scale, CCPR was engaged in a virtual world software development project:

The idea here is that you would have a customizable virtual simulation training game that would target players all along the emergency response hierarchy from first responders to agency decision makers. Since the game would be customizable, you could put GIS and building data on every structure in NYC. This interface would then function not merely as a training tool but it would also be of use in the event of an actual catastrophe response.[76]

At another level of scale, CCPR focused on architec-turally-designed training spaces that integrated real and virtual components to simulate events, such as the one operated by the NYC Fire Department and the National Emergency Management Association (NEMA):

> We visited the NYC Fire Department training campus on Randall's Island last week, where they have a bunch of regular classrooms, and then they have a two- to three-block long street scene, like a Hollywood movie set, in which all the different Manhattan building types are represented. In a training exercise, the trainees pull up to the set and there is a guy in a tower who controls what happens, from pyrotechnics to walls falling down, etc. This is the kind of thing that needs to be developed and effectively integrated into the training and development of all emergency responder personnel, and special care needs to be taken to ensure that individuals and organizations have the right kind of incentives to use the facilities.[77]

At a much broader level of scale, another example of inte-grated experience cited by CCPR is TOPOFF, a series of catastrophe response exercises coordinated nationally by NEMA involving all the 'top officials' who would

---

[76] Source: personal interview.
[77] Source: personal interview.

participate in the consequence management of terrorist attacks. The first three major exercises took place in 2000, when key personnel simulated a plague attack in Denver, a mustard gas attack in Portsmouth, New Hampshire, and a radiation leak in Washington DC. The second set of exercises, TOPOFF 2, was conducted in 2003, with 18,000 people from 103 US government agencies and 19 Canadian departments participating in seven different exercises, including scenarios such as weapons of mass destruction attacks, cyberterrorism attacks, dirty bombs in metropolitan areas, and additional chemical and radiation attacks. CCPR staff paid close attention to the findings from these simulations that were presented at the NEMA Conference on September 9, 2003, including the assertions that 'the speed of decision making was often outpaced by the tempo of the news' and that 'changes in the HSAS [Homeland Security Alert System] to "red" have significant economic and social implications that have not yet been completely explored.'[78]

---

[78] Source documentation provided to authors by CCPR. For additional information on the simulations in question, cf. http://www.ojp. usdoj.gov/odp/library/bulletins.htm. As for the opinions of CCPR staff about the various factors constraining the effectiveness of such simulations, consider the following quote: 'The thing to keep in mind about these TOPOFF findings is that they emerged in and through the physical experience, on behalf of thousands of participants, of a simulated catastrophe. In that respect they are valuable and revealing of the ways in which the conditions faced directly by first responders might change depending on how they are reported on and understood by people far from the front lines. But in the event of a real catastrophe, the potential parameters for variability are even greater. For example ... "in the event of bio terror attack, 30–40% of health care providers won't show up to work. So the lessons learned from TOPOFF need to be evaluated in that light, where the viability of the response strategy depends directly on ensuring that the 60 to 70% of responders who will in fact show up have been through the drill and know more or less what physical activities they might be called upon to perform" ' (source: personal interview).

Thus as CCPR staff engaged both in the development of virtual gaming environments, as well as in the development and refinement of scenario training drills, they recognized the importance of creating preparedness training processes that integrated as much as possible of the catastrophe experience into the daily reality of the organizations responsible for preparedness.

We believe that these activities played a significant role in CCPR's attempts to learn from past experiences and identify opportunities to become more strategically prepared for similarly catastrophic events in the future.

13.4   First-order reflections: learning from the front line

Reflecting more broadly on all three of CCPR's activity patterns at once, we believe that they provide initial indications of how practical wisdom might be developed in organizations. To the extent that CCPR's storytelling activity addresses both past experiences as well as hypothetical future experiences in which people in organizations confront the limits of the thinkable and the possible, it provides a (relatively, in comparison to a repeat of the catastrophic experience itself) safe frame within which people in organizations can experiment with the balances characteristic of the dynamic model of practical wisdom. With specific regard to the balances, CCPR's activity involving dialogue with diverse groups of people appears not only as a calculated attempt to derive input from diverse sources relevant to a unified, clearly defined problem, but also as involving an interpretative framing and re-framing of the challenge of preparedness itself in view of the interests of different constituencies. This balance was skewed deliberately by the 'one million casualties' story, where the interest was distributed among a practically infinite number of constituencies. Finally, with respect to the exposure to (and variation of) the dynamisms, the activity focused on integrated experience appears to be a direct, embodied experimentation with those media in and through which preparedness is both perceived and enacted.

We believe that CCPR's activities provide indications of how practical wisdom might be developed not only 'at the front lines' of catastrophe preparedness, but additionally in more generic organizational situations. If we take a step back, we find, for example, that within management studies and practice there is an entire field urging managers to pay more attention to the power of storytelling for effective communication and learning. Similarly, there has been great deal of related attention focused by researchers, as well as practitioners, on the importance of dialogue in organizations as a model for conflict resolution, sensemaking, and learning. Finally, there is another long-standing tradition in strategic management that involves scenario development, simulation, and gaming as methods of both eliciting and exercising the skills and resource capacities needed in the face of uncertainty. Our suggestion is simply that these existing traditions of management development can be re-framed as methods of developing practical wisdom.

13.5   Second-order reflections: encouraging the habit

Reflecting on the CCPR data, as well as the preceding indications from management theory, we suggest that one particularly effective method of developing practical wisdom, if indeed any activity can complement or improve on lived experience itself, is the telling of tales, the sharing of stories.

Beyond the informational content of the story itself, narrative structures include latent (and sometimes disruptive) assumptions about time, causation, and morality.

To the extent that narratives are dramatic, leading from a beginning through a transformation to an end, they present means/ends relationships for discussion and interpretation. To the extent that narratives testify to the virtues of the dramatis personae (for example, the hero's journey) the story provides an occasion to reflect on morality.[79] Of course, the story may function more or less effectively in this way, insofar as the story itself remains contingent on the historical and material circumstances in which it is told.

In order for the normative question of whether 'the hero' did the right thing to be posed reflectively (that is, what would you have done? what would I have done?), storytelling additionally requires a context for interpretation and critical dialogue. In this sense, the importance of diversity among the group of people in dialogue with each other appears not just as a moral good in itself (as it is often depicted, and may well be), but also as a tactically effective means of assuring that the community has requisite variety sufficient to deal with the uncertain threat in the environment.

And yet, even though a well-told tale can provide an occasion for critical discussion and reflection in a community of people, talk can be cheap in comparison to the pedagogical value of integrated, embodied experience.

---

[79]At a more micro-level of narrative analysis, the moral, ethical import or significance of narrative can be presented in condensed form by proverbs, maxims, and principles which read as little phrases that tell a story and provide moral justification and encouragement for a particular form of action. With maxims, the normativity tends to be a little more ambiguous than with commandments, but this range only illustrates the extent to which practical wisdom may or may not be taught prescriptively. On this point, we have pursued a line of inquiry pertaining to 'simple guiding principles' (cf. D. Oliver and J. Roos (2005) 'Decision-Making in High-Velocity Environments: The Importance of Guiding Principles', *Organization Studies* (26) 6: 889–913).

In this light, we find it no accident that the military, required to deal with such radical risk and uncertainty, engages in an endless series of drills and repetitions to train the minds and bodies of those individuals who may be required to confront the limits of the thinkable and the possible.[80]

In light of these reflections, we suggest that the CCPR activities have a direct, normative implication for organizational leaders and managers confronting the challenge of preparedness in the face of catastrophic as well as mundane circumstances. To phrase this implication in terms of advice: *if you're going to try to develop practical wisdom as a way to hedge against the asymmetric threat potential that stretches the organization beyond the limits of knowledge and action, then you should strategically develop practices involving storytelling, dialogue, and integrated experiences at all levels of the organization.*

We leave this claim open to debate, particularly because we recognize that the three different activities undertaken by CCPR during the phase of their activity during which we were gathering data can hardly be considered a complete compendium of the ways in which practical wisdom might be developed in organizations. Furthermore, we recognize that the case data concerning the activities undertaken by a federally-funded research and educational institute may not necessarily be indicative of how other, more traditional private-sector organizations could or should respond to the strategic challenge of preparedness. And yet, on the basis of our own ongoing research in the domain of strategic management studies, we suggest that the three activities outlined above point

---

[80] On this point, the US military's after-action review (AAR) practice appears as a further attempt to combine integrated, embodied experience with storytelling and open dialogue.

toward a more general category of activity that extends clearly beyond the horizons of the preparedness field, and has broad implications for the development of human cognitive, social, emotional, and perceptual capacities in organizations, namely: *play*.

14.0
The Importance of Play in Organizations

The fact that CCPR engaged in activities such as story-telling, dialogue and integrated experience appears neither accidental nor unique to the field of catastrophe pre-paredness. Our research indicates that from Aristotle's time onward, attempts to develop the virtuous habit of practical wisdom have relied on such pedagogical methods. As we will see, the activity of play itself may be the most natural way for people in organizations to develop practical wisdom.

14.1 Again, ancient roots

It is well known that Aristotle affirmed the cathartic function of tragic drama as a way to develop ethical character among citizens in a democracy. He maintained that this narrative art provided a way for people to experience and learn from suffering – for example, the suffering of Oedipus, who unwittingly killed his father (cf. Figure 8: Squander) and slept with his mother (cf. Figure 7: Blow-back) – without actually having to undergo the experience itself.

Of course, the use of drama as a pedagogical technique remains subject to criticism, insofar as some narrative forms appear to develop questionable patterns of moral discernment. Indeed, the question about films such as *The Day after Tomorrow* is precisely whether they develop or erode the capacity for ethical responses to catastrophic events among the general movie-viewing public. It is not our aim to settle such questions, but instead to indicate the extent to which *storytelling*, as a narrative practice, *has a significant history as a playful method of developing practical wisdom.*

Plato, Aristotle's intellectual forebear, saw the proliferation of such questions (that is, 'if *The Day after Tomorrow* doesn't particularly help develop practical wisdom in the field of preparedness, then what about *Apollo 13*? Or for that matter, *Star Wars?*') as an indication of the limits of the pedagogical function of narrative.[81] He affirmed dialogue instead as the method most proper to the development of practical wisdom. In this sense, CCPR's practice of engaging in dialogue with diverse groups of people has a time-honored precedent in Socrates' habit of standing around the marketplace engaging in dialogue with all and sundry. And as tiresome as his interlocutors may have found him, his signature method of philosophical inquiry, 'Socratic dialogue', was explicitly understood as a form of 'serious play'.[82]

---

[81] For the record, Plato famously cast the poets out of his *Republic* for precisely this reason: that poetry can be used to cultivate vice just as easily as it can be used to cultivate virtue. Ask yourself: are you more given to reciting Wordsworth or dirty limericks?

[82] For a general account of the playful dynamics in the Platonic texts, cf. Bernard Freydberg's excellent book *The Play of the Platonic Dialogues* (1997). As we here refer to 'wisdom', we should recognize the long-standing and ongoing tradition of debate within Platonic scholarship about the degree and nature of overlap between theoretical wisdom (*sophia*) and practical wisdom (*phronesis*). The most common argument,

Indeed, while the various texts written by Plato provide significant historical evidence of how such dialogical activities may have unfolded in ancient Athens, within the texts themselves there is explicit counsel never to mistake written accounts of wisdom for wisdom itself, nor to assume that reading a written dialogue could ever be as effective in the development of wisdom as the experiential and playful process of practicing the dialectical method of inquiry.[83]

The importance of play for the development of wisdom is affirmed even more explicitly (and famously) in the *Republic*, where Socrates insists that the pedagogical methods most suited to the development of the practical wisdom necessary for a well-governed state were *music* and *gymnastic*. We need only to broaden our understanding of 'gymnastics' beyond the modern Olympic sports to include all manner of physical training, including the operation of machines and technologies, to see that the activities undertaken by CCPR involving narrative and integrated

---

supported typically with evidence from the *Symposium* and the *Republic*, is that Plato (and to some extent, Socrates) believed in a sharp distinction between the two, insofar as they pertain respectively to the world of ideas and the world of appearances. A counter-argument, supported typically with evidence from the *Sophist*, the *Theaetetus*, and sometimes the *Parmenides*, is that Socrates himself should be understood as a simple teacher of ethics, practicing the dialectic in concrete and contingent historical circumstances – and on such an interpretation, the much-vaunted 'theory of ideas' reads less as a metaphysical theory and more as a direct, tactical intervention (i) on Socrates' part, into the dogmatic slumbers of his conversation partner, Glaucon, and (ii) on Plato's part, into the wine-sloshed Athenian polis (cf. James Davidson (1997), *Courtesans and Fishcakes: The Consuming Passions of Classical Athens*).

[83] This point is made most clearly in the *Phaedrus*, where Socrates walks outside the city with his friend Phaedrus and jokes about how foolish people are to think that what is written down *as* philosophy actually *is* philosophy.

experiences can be understood generically as forms of serious play.

14.2 Again, modern vestiges: theoretical and empirical evidence

It may seem at first somewhat paradoxical to suggest that play is an appropriate way to deal with circumstances at the limits of what is thinkable and possible. And yet, for military commanders accustomed to dealing with overwhelming uncertainty and asymptotic threats, the experience of war gaming is familiar enough. While certain traditions of playful education continue to thrive to some extent in our educational systems,[84] they remain most prominent in organizational settings characterized by extreme uncertainty, such as war and long-term corporate strategy. In this sense, the history of scenario planning itself can be seen as an extended and ongoing engagement in the playful practice of integrated experience as a way to develop practical wisdom.

But at the risk of discovering only what may seem obvious already (that is, that corporate strategists often borrow analytic and training techniques from the military), we should summarize the line of argument that we are unfolding at this point:

1 CCPR's activities have significant roots in contemporary management theory and practice, beyond the narrow sub-field of catastrophe preparedness;
2 these roots extend back to ancient Greece, where such activities were explicitly affirmed as methods of developing practical wisdom;

---

[84] For example, Montessori, Steiner schools, the Rhodes 'scholar-athlete' ideal inherited from the British prep school cultivation of sport, and so on.

3 in both ancient and modern times, these activities have been meaningfully characterized as forms of play; and
4 therefore play can contribute to the development of practical wisdom in organizations.

From 2000 to 2006 we, together with colleagues at the Imagination Lab Foundation explored the practical relevance of play for imaginative, effective, and responsible management practices. Specifically, we found considerable theoretical and empirical support for the notion that organizations can generate more innovative strategy content if they make their strategy processes more hands-on and playful (Roos, Victor and Statler, 2004; Roos, 2006).

This proposition arises out of the vast research on play that has been undertaken in different academic fields. Psychologists have long argued that play develops the capacity for logical operations and cognitive processes (Piaget, 1958), as well as the capacity to understand meaning in culturally-specific contexts (Vygotsky, 1978). Psychotherapists have in turn explored play (and the creative arts) as a method of therapeutic intervention suitable for children as well as adults that encourages the development of a capacity to create meaning in difficult and ambiguous transitional spaces (Winnicott, 1971). Social theorists have argued more broadly that through play individuals become familiar with societal symbols, identify themselves in relation to others, and acquire skills to function effectively in the community (Mead, 2001). Lest we assume that social contexts are simply given to play, rather than also produced by it, we recall that play has contributed to the formation of civilization as such, influencing and giving rise to institutions like war, law, art, and philosophy (Huizinga, 1950).

In view of these (and many other) literature streams, we remain particularly compelled by the notion that the activity of play can serve as *'the primary place for the expression of anything that is humanly imaginable'* precisely because it is not saddled with the requirement to produce anything (Sutton-Smith, 1997: 226). Moreover, precisely because expressive play activities involve cognitive, social and emotional dimensions of experience they encourage the *'potentiation of adaptive variability'* (ibid.: 231).

In view of these arguments, we have framed our experimentation with playful strategy work as *serious play*, that is, as a playful mode of activity that (i) incorporates the cognitive, social, and emotional dimensions posited in the literature, and (ii) remains intentionally open to emergent change.[85] Within this frame, we experimented with play-based strategy practices involving over 1000 managers from dozens of different organizations. These experiments put particular emphasis on play that uses three-dimensional media to craft and make sense of strategic challenges.[86] But what is it exactly about play that recommends it as an activity through which practical wisdom may be developed? We can now answer this question in direct reference to the dynamic model of practical wisdom we introduced above.

---

[85]Additional dimensions of serious play developed in Roos (2006) include spontaneity, emotions, and drama.

[86]P. Burgi, C. Jacobs and J. Roos (2005) 'From Metaphor to Practice in the Crafting of Strategy,' *Journal of Management Inquiry,* 14(1): 78–94. For more on the importance of using the hands in strategic sensemaking processes, cf. also M. Statler, C. Jacobs and J. Roos (2006) 'Performing Strategy: Analogical Reasoning as Strategic Practice', *Academy of Management Annual Conference Best Paper Proceedings.*

14.3   Play and practical wisdom

As far as the limits of the thinkable and the possible are concerned, the most important thing about play is the extent to which it involves an engagement with ambiguity. Following the work of Sutton-Smith (1997), we can see that because people at play are confronted with ambiguity and yet not necessarily required to produce anything in response to it, they are thereby able to imagine and enact anything that is humanly possible. And within this range of possibility for action is enabled the variety necessary for adaptive responses to develop. In this light, play provides a concrete method of simulating the transgression of the limits of both the thinkable and the possible.

In Figure 12, play appears as a zone for action and reflection in which an increase in the need for preparedness is simulated. By simulating this increased need, organizations can explore the limits of what is thinkable and possible and still remain safe from the immediate risk of over-whelming, real-world consequences. In playful activities our temporal horizons, as well as our interests and our forms of response, may be deliberately constrained or altered so that new patterns of strategic thought or action can be creatively enacted.

With respect to the dynamisms outlined in our model of practical wisdom (Figure 11), we can now say that serious play involves: (i) a mode of intentionality attuned to the emergent possible, (ii) a fluid engagement with the milieu, involving holistic operations within an ambiguous frame, and (iii) an opportunity to integrate multi- and mixed-media into a strategic sensemaking process.

So, then, if indeed play does provide an activity through which practical wisdom may be developed in organizations, a number of questions remain about how play might be operationalized within organizational settings. Our own experiments provide some indications of how strategic

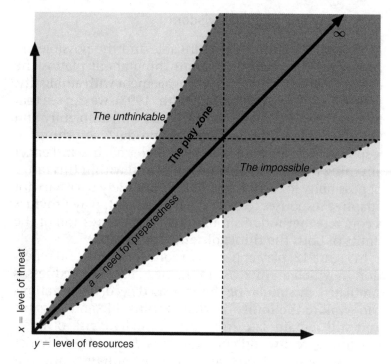

Figure 12   The play zone

practice can be seen as an opportunity to develop practical wisdom through serious play. But more generally, how might playful activities be used to cultivate the virtuous habit of practical wisdom among managers?

15.0
Seeking New Directions in Management Education

Just as Aristotle's 'Lyceum' served as the place for deliberation about the role of practical wisdom for statesmen in ancient Athens, we believe the modern-day business school is the best place to deliberate about practical wisdom in organizations. And just as Aristotle assumed that the social world was so complex that practical wisdom (and not just science or cunning) was required for leaders, we suggest that organizations faced with the need for preparedness will benefit if managers increasingly reflect on and cultivate practical wisdom.

Since the late 1990s, almost every business school in the world has revisited, rejuvenated, or totally re-invented its approach to business education. Thus, in spite of the dominant logic that presupposes the primacy of scientific intelligence over wisdom for managerial decision-making, there have been a number of prominent suggestions concerning how to reframe the process, as well as the intended outcomes, of management education. In the following section, we would like to highlight those initiatives that are coherent with our model of practical wisdom.

Henry Mintzberg has taken perhaps the most dramatic and widely publicized steps in the direction of reframing

management education as a practical art.[87] Working
together with a number of academic colleagues and practicing managers, and explicitly distancing himself from
the MBA model, Mintzberg has spearheaded a program
called the International Masters in Practicing Management
(IMPM). The basic premise for this program is that management is a practice rather than a science. At a process
level, the program includes apprenticeships, internships,
on-the-job learning, mentoring, exchange programs – all
wrapped in cycles of action and reflection that explicitly
include the normative or ethical dimensions of organizational life. These process elements overlap significantly
with the integrated experience, dialogue, and storytelling
that we identified at the front lines in the case of CCPR
and analysed as forms of play that cultivate practical
wisdom.

In spite of all the effort to integrate action and reflection, Mintzberg maintains on the dust jacket of his recent
book that he is 'not the dean of a business school', thus
distinguishing between his role as a faculty member and
the practice of administration. Although this lack of
direct self-identification with the organizational leadership role may cast doubt on the ethics and effectiveness
of the program design itself, it may equally serve as evidence of Mintzberg's efforts to balance specific dynamics
intrinsic to the milieu of academic administration. In any
case, Mintzberg's recommendations have been supported
by people who have accepted the practical challenge of
leading a business school, for example, Laura D'Andrea
Tyson, Dean of London Business School, and Nigel

---

[87] Henry Mintzberg (2004), *Managers Not MBA's: A Hard Look at the Soft
Practice of Managing and Management Development* (Berrett-Koehler
Publishers: San Francisco).

Andrews, a governor of LBS and a venture partner at the Internet Capital Group.[88] These educators explicitly acknowledge the interest that LBS has in maintaining its competitive viability as a resource for large organizations in need of training and education. They appear to accept as a matter of fact that business is global in scope. They also appear to presuppose an asymmetric threat potential, as it is driven by uncertainty in that global environment.

Working with these apparent assumptions, they conducted 100 interviews with 'executives from global companies' seeking information about what sort of skills executives require, and in turn, what LBS can do in order to meet those educational and training needs. What they found merits full quotation:

> The corporate leaders we interviewed indeed produced an extensive list of qualities they desired in future recruits, but almost none involved functional or technical knowledge. Rather, virtually all their requirements could be summed up as follows: *the need for more thoughtful, more aware, more sensitive, more flexible, more adaptive managers, capable of being molded and developed into global executives.* (2004; our italics)

We interpret this list of needs as a sketch, from the perspective of a business school dean, of the practices that must be habituated over the course of the business education. Indeed their data suggest that, among top executives, the goal and outcome of education is becoming more processual, more 'action oriented' *and* more ethical:

> Business education must become more action oriented, but also must find ways to nurture integrity,

---

[88] L. Tyson, and N. Andrews (2004), 'The Upwardly Global MBA', *Strategy + Business* (Autumn): 67.

judgment and intuition – a seemingly contradictory mandate that schools nevertheless must learn to prosecute. (2004)

This contradictory mandate appears to map directly to the importance of practical wisdom for dealing with the problem of preparedness as we have described it. At the limits of what is possible for action, organizations have a need for ethically-based judgment and action.[89]

How, then, should business schools 'prosecute the mandate' of developing practical wisdom in order to help global organizations be more prepared for the unexpected? According to LBS Dean Tyson, the answers lie in reframing the case method, making it less theoretical and more action-oriented. They acknowledge that 'judgment and intuition are developed through repeated experience' (2004). In an effort to provide that habituation necessary for the development of practical wisdom, they advocate (i) the development of shorter-term, more experiential 'case simulations', (ii) international educational exchange, (iii) apprenticeship-style 'shadowing', where business students follow executives over the course of a day, and (iv) internships. These different practices appear to provide 'playful' (that is, experientially rich exposures to ambiguity, yet without the direct consequences of an unexpected event) habituation to the ethical challenges of management in a global and uncertain environment.

Tyson and Andrews define this virtue of comportment as 'acting ethically in accordance with values', but they leave unanswered questions about how those values can and should be shaped, much less what in fact they are, in actual cases of business (or business educational) practice.

---

[89] An open question: what is LBS's own ethical stance as it confronts the limits of what it can think and do?

Ian Mitroff and Diane Swanson, however, maintain perhaps more rigorously that business decisions cannot ever be considered 'value-free', even when the values themselves are not apparently contested, as in the extreme case of the need for preparedness. Mitroff is one of the most prominent researchers focused on crisis management and strategy, and Swanson has founded a *Business Ethics Education Initiative* that seeks to monitor best practices in ethics education across business degree programs, while providing research and advisory support to business educators.

Mitroff and Swanson insist that in order to develop such a capacity for ethical judgment and action, the business educational experience must not only be more fully integrated with the world of organizational practice, but additionally it must draw on up-to-date sources of information about ethics, rather than relying on stale dichotomies inherited from theories that have subsequently been repudiated in philosophy (2004).

Stewart Clegg and Anne Ross-Smith have taken up the challenge that Mitroff and Swanson describe, and explicitly introduced the concept of practical wisdom into the debate about how management education should be transformed in an increasingly global and uncertain world, where preparedness is required (2001). They argue reflectively that the ethical dimension of business education extends to include the researchers and educators themselves. At this level, the challenge of performative enactment is raised:

> Postpositivist, philosophically-oriented writing is both a good element in a more pluralist management academy and a signpost to a future management academy more vigorously engaged, one which takes stances on ethical and political matters in a way that positivist work shuns. (Clegg and Ross-Smith, 2003: 96)

Or more broadly phrased, management education should presume that management is, itself, a kind of phronesis or practical wisdom, a discipline 'that is pragmatic, variable, context dependent, based on practical rationality, leading not to a concern with generating formal covering law-like explanations but to building contextual, case-based knowledge' (ibid.: 86).

Reviewing these recent proposals for how to advance management education, we find that Mintzberg has mapped the new terrain perhaps most comprehensively at the level of practice, and that the London Business School is following suit in its own way. In turn, crisis management expert Mitroff is arguing that ethics should be integrated more comprehensively into management education, and Clegg and Ross-Smith state explicitly that the purpose of management education should be to develop practical wisdom.

Ghoshal's (2005) recent and harsh critique of business schools can be framed as a lack of practical wisdom: '*Without that wisdom it is not surprising that, when we are in doubt, we do not necessarily do the "right" thing*' (Roos, 2006: 233). With his reference to the 'pretense of knowledge' (2005: 77) Ghoshal recognizes that management knowledge must be more than the natural science-inspired causal explanations that dominate mainstream business school teaching, just as Aristotle recognized that leaders need more than *episteme*. Ghoshal's wish to move beyond the all-encompassing pessimistic assumptions of management theory, which '*curb managers' ability to play out a more positive role in society*' (2005: 82), supports Aristotle's notion that leaders must consider the common good of their society. Overall, Ghoshal helps us see that the need for values in strategic management practice may be exacerbated because business schools tend to teach amoral theories that free the students '*from any sense of moral responsibility*' (200: 76).

Extrapolating from Ghoshal's critique, we suggest that MBA programs should purposefully be designed and delivered to cultivate participants' practical wisdom. A design principle might be to consider the MBA program as a unique opportunity for co-learning among open-minded *participants* with experience of management practice and equally open-minded *faculty* with experience of trans-disciplinary practice-oriented research. Unlike undergraduate and PhD programs, MBA programs as well as executive education programs provide the opportunity for such co-learning, especially if participants have a few years' managerial experience before attempting an MBA. The hallmark of such co-learning processes will be dialogue rather than just monologue, constructivism rather than just instructionism, and multi-sensory experience rather than just intellectualizing (Roos, 2006).[90]

With respect to the conceptual framework of practical wisdom, as well as with respect to the practical pedagogy of play, including storytelling, dialogue, and integrated experience as well as drama, these various recent proposals and critiques of business school curricula appear to

---

[90] After this manuscript was completed Johan joined Stockholm School of Economics (SSE) as Dean of MBA Programs. Founded in 1909, until 2006 SSE offered the Germanic-Nordic four-year 'civilekonom' degree program and PhD programs in economics and business administration. During 2007 SEE aligned with the so-called Bologna model into three-year BSc, two-year MSc, and three-year PhD programs. As an integral part of its executive education activities over the last decade SSE gradually offered highly ranked (part-time) Executive MBA programs in Stockholm, Riga, St Petersburg and Moscow, but did not launch a full-time, one-year MBA program until 2004. Johan's aspiration is to make increased practical wisdom a primary learning objective of SSE MBA programs and, thereby, inspire others to continually innovate the curriculum and learning process of this important degree program.

provide additional support for our interpretation of the CCPR findings, as well as further indication of how practical wisdom might be cultivated in organizations through management development.

In short, we believe that the habit of practical wisdom *can* be cultivated in organizations as a response to the need for preparedness. Specifically, we have found that:

1 storytelling, dialogue, and integrated experience are practices that can be found on the 'front lines' of the post-9/11 catastrophe preparedness field;
2 from a historical perspective, these practices are deeply rooted in human experience, and can be collectively referred to as forms of play;
3 such playful activities can be integrated into management education in such a way as to contribute to the development of practical wisdom in organizations.

In the following pages, we will outline the implications of these conclusions for the emerging preparedness field, and for the practice of strategic management.

16.0
Practical Wisdom as Everyday Strategic Preparedness

The argument that we have presented thus far can be summarized as follows:

- in a world characterized by complexity and uncertainty, organizations are forced to deal with the strategic challenge of preparedness;
- dealing with this challenge requires people in organizations not only to gather knowledge and develop capabilities for action, but, additionally, to allow their decisions and actions to be guided by ethical values;
- practical wisdom provides a framework that describes how strategists and leaders can balance ethical demands with demands for practical effectiveness;
- practical wisdom can be developed in organizations through playful activities such as storytelling, dialogue, and integrated experience.

In accordance with Aristotle's notion of the happiness (*eudaimonia*) that is characteristic of the well-managed household (*oikonomia*), we suggest furthermore that when wisdom is developed in practice, it can have positive effects not only in the surprise event of a catastrophe, but additionally in the everyday circumstances of organizational life. Thus the title of this book: *we propose that practical wisdom, defined as a human capacity to deal effectively and ethically with unexpected change, contributes to 'everyday strategic preparedness' in organizations.*

In this sense, our dynamic model of practical wisdom sheds light on the various factors that contribute to preparedness on an ongoing, everyday basis, while our reflections on the case of CCPR and the concept of serious play shed light on how people in organizations can develop preparedness in the course of their everyday activities. In the interest of cultivating this potential for wise practice among strategy scholars and practitioners, we now offer a series of reflections for researchers in the field of management and organizational studies, and a series of recommendations for people in the preparedness field.

17.0
Reflecting on the Field of Management and Organizational Studies

Having proposed that practical wisdom contributes to everyday strategic preparedness in organizations, we should at this point outline the research agenda that this proposition calls for within the field of management and organizational studies.

With 'practical wisdom', we have not identified a better mousetrap, crafted a new tool, discovered a better algorithm, designed a more efficient system, arrived at a more necessary conclusion, or revealed a truth of strategic management that is truer than all the rest. We have instead developed a conceptual framework that can be used to describe those cases in which people deal appropriately with unexpected change by creatively enacting the common good. And we have argued that, in such cases, strategists and organizational leaders who are practically wise can respond ethically and effectively to the strategic challenge of preparedness in specific organizational contexts.

We recognize that, in one sense, the research on which we base this claim remains at a very early stage. Following the traditional, positivist model of social science, we remain strictly speaking at the 'theory development' stage, far from the empirical testing of hypotheses and the production of validated, statistically generalizable findings. Indeed, from such a methodological perspective, this entire book may serve only as a very preliminary overview of the various factors relevant to the study of practical wisdom in organizational contexts. Following our dynamic model these factors include balances of interests, responses to the environment, and time horizons – as well as the mode of intentionality, the medium of communication, and the cultural and historical milieu in which the actions take place.

Of course, in another sense, we have shown that scholarly interest in practical wisdom stretches back thousands of years, from ancient Greece through to present-day philosophy and psychology. And recalling Aristotle's distinction between science and practical wisdom, strictly speaking it may be methodologically impossible to generate knowledge about human social interaction that has the same predictive validity as knowledge about the natural, physical world. From this perspective, this book may serve as nothing more and nothing less than an occasion for reflection and debate (among those people who read it) about those habits of mind and body that appear to contribute to 'the good' in organizations where people struggle with the strategic challenge of preparedness.

In any case, we acknowledge that in order to 'prove' our proposition that practical wisdom leads to everyday strategic preparedness in organizations, additional argumentation can hardly suffice. Instead, an entire research agenda needs to be developed and pursued. What questions and methods should guide this agenda?

The dynamic model of practical wisdom directs attention to the individual-level decisions and actions that performatively strike balances of time horizons, interests, and responses to the environment. And yet at the same time, it directs attention to societal- and cultural-level factors that both enable and constrain individual decision-making processes. In this sense, the questions guiding the research agenda focused on practical wisdom in organizations should address the interplay between and among these distinct 'levels of analysis'. More polemically, we suggest that strategic preparedness will not be understood by organizational researchers unless the epistemological distinctions between individual-, group- and organizational-level variables are deliberately, albeit carefully, broken down and reconstructed in a theory of strategy practice that presupposes a dynamic, process ontology (cf. Tsoukas and Chia, 2002; Clegg et al., 2005).

Beyond the practical need for strategic preparedness in organizations, we identify a need within the field of management and organization studies for greater understanding of those specific practices of mind and body that are associated with practical wisdom. For example, speaking about different, diverging, and even competing human interests, what, exactly, is a *balance*? Inspired by Aristotle again: how might the three balances we have identified relate to each other, in terms of a 'golden mean'? How might the cultivation of such a golden mean involve an additional balance, at the level of the mode of intentionality, between control and flexibility? How might the capacity for control and flexibility be impacted by the presence or absence of the different media available for embodied expression and experience? How might the meaning of embodied experience itself change over time – or, more provocatively, is there some universal, a priori intrinsic or irreducible value to human experience or not?

We pose these open, philosophical questions directly to the academic community of strategy researchers. We furthermore suggest that as strategic management scholars, we must consider questions such as these if we seek to better understand that form of intelligent action which enables people to respond both in extreme and everyday circumstances to the unexpected. Indeed, we may not understand the judgments and actions that take place in organizations at the limits of the thinkable and the possible unless we ourselves push the limits of what is thinkable and possible within our own academic organizations.

In an effort precisely to push these limits, we identify two streams of contemporary organizational scholarship where a robust, holistic theoretical basis for research on practical wisdom is being collectively elaborated: the 'strategy-as-practice' research community,[91] and the 'organizational aesthetics' research community.[92]

As a response to the questions above about how the interplay between individual-, group- and organizational-level factors might be dealt with as an integrated phenomenon unto itself, we find it appropriate first to cite the statement of purpose on the Strategy-as-Practice community website in its entirety:

> Strategy as Practice is a community of scholars interested in the practice of strategy. As scholars we are interested in a broad spectrum of issues concerned with the making and doing of strategy and strategic change in organisations. We apply a variety of different theoretical approaches, such as practice perspectives on organisations, sensemaking, discourse analysis, and script theory. What we are agreed on is the importance of a focus on the processes and practices constituting the everyday activities of organizational life and relating to strategic

---

[91] Cf. http://www.strategy-as-practice.org/ Cf. Orlikowski (2000); Balogun, Huff and Johnson (2003); Hendry and Seidl (2003); Heracleous (2003); Jarzabkowski (2004); Johnson, Melin and Whittington (2003); Régner (2003); Whittington (2002).

[92] Cf. AACORN – the Arts, Aesthetics, Creativity & Organization Research Network (http://aacorn.net/index.htm); also, the Art of Management and Organization Conference series organized by the Essex Management Centre. (http://www.essex.ac.uk/AFM/emc/second_art_of_management_and_org.shtm)

outcomes, if we are to move our field forward. We see the linkage through to strategic outcomes as an important component of our research as we ultimately need to be able to link the outcomes of (multiple) strategising activities, events and behaviours within the firm to more macro organisational, institutional and, possibly, even broader social contexts and outcomes. If we are to theorise about the link between what occurs within organisations and more macro levels of analysis we need to situate organisational activities within the broader context of action. As such, we share with traditional strategy research a concern for firm performance, but we also emphasise the significance of potentially multiple strategizing outcomes and their interactions through time. As a result, we are typically involved in in-depth qualitative research that enables us to examine the inside of strategising processes, and marry the concern for both content and process, and for both intentional and emergent activities and outcomes. In addition, we acknowledge the role of a broad range of strategists outside of the senior management team in organisations, and the potential impact of others within the field on strategising activities, such as consultants and business school academics.[93]

At the level of its research questions, this community acknowledges that an integrated concept of practice includes elements that have traditionally been isolated as subjective, inter-subjective, and objective. Specifically, the phenomenon of practice includes a notion of agency that corresponds to the familiar concept of subjective volition (that is, the 'will'). But it also includes a notion of structure that corresponds to the quasi-objective factors

---

[93] (http://www.strategy-as-practice.org/), accessed August 3, 2005.

that constrain and enable the exercise of volition and choice in concrete circumstances for action. In this sense, the traditional dichotomy that distinguishes free will from determinism blurs significantly, and all human action appears to contain aspects or elements of both freedom and fate.

From a strategic organizational perspective (no less than a political perspective), our question then becomes: how can the circumstances for individual action be designed or shaped so that individual choices are exercised in ways that contribute to, rather than detract from, preparedness? More broadly phrased: what are the social, historical, and cultural circumstances that appear to enable (rather than constrain) practically wise responses to unexpected change?[94] Or, more inductively phrased, to acknowledge the empirical variability of the phenomenon in question: what exactly are people doing when organizations say they are becoming more prepared?

The community of organizational researchers interested in aesthetics has begun to develop innovative ways to address questions such as these. Based on the aesthetic philosophy of Immanuel Kant and Friedrich Schiller, researchers in this field[95] identify 'aesthetics' precisely in terms of a play between formal structure and material

---

[94] Directions for possible future research in this regard can be found not only within management and organization studies (cf. Gary Hamel's 'Quest for Resilience', Harvard Business School Press, 2003; or Paul Light's notion of 'robustness' in *The Four Pillars of High Performance*, New York: McGraw Hill 2004), but also in population ecology (cf. Jared Diamond, *Collapse: How Societies Choose to Fail or Succeed*, New York: Viking 2004) and political philosophy (Paolo Virno, *Grammar of the Multitude*, New York: Semiotexte 2004).

[95] Cf. especially Guillet de Monthoux, (2004); Strati, (1999); Kirkeby (2003); Linstead and Hopfl (2000); and the *Human Relations* special issue on 'Organizing Aesthetics', 55 (7 July 2002). See also Taylor and Hanson (2005).

contents of human experience. Furthermore, they orient (especially following the phenomenology of Merleau-Ponty) toward those aspects of human experience that are primarily relational, rather than individual. In this light, the arts appear not just as a frivolous diversion from the bottom-line concerns of organizations, but instead as a meaningful example of how people might strike balances through aesthetic play. Thus strategic management scholars seeking greater understanding of practical wisdom under conditions of uncertainty can learn from the long-standing tradition of debate within philosophy and critical theory about the relationship between aesthetic judgment and moral judgment.

These two emerging streams of research help us to formulate the research questions that we believe must be addressed. They also raise additional questions, relevant to any search for greater understanding, about the methods of study that are appropriate to the phenomenon in question.

Looking back at where we started this book, it appears that the trend of movement within strategic management from a static ontology toward a dynamic ontology has directed attention toward the 'soft' factors (for example, intentionality, affect, and so on) that contribute, alongside the balance sheet, to firm performance. In line with this trend, strategic management scholars have repeatedly called for the development of qualitative research techniques and other, alternative methods of scientific understanding.[96] However, the overwhelming bias within the

---

[96] In the *Strategic Management Journal* alone, such calls have echoed for more than a decade with little response: guest editors Chakravarthy and Doz focused on the notion of 'self-renewal' for the field (1992); Pettigrew sought to identify a series of new 'fundamental themes' (1992); and Prahalad and Hamel searched explicitly for 'new paradigms' (1994).

field continues to privilege measurement and prediction – and this dominant logic[97] is sustained by journal editors, tenure review committees, and other entrenched systems of reward and punishment within the academy. In this regard, we state explicitly our belief that although it will never be possible to develop a predictive science of what is ethically good, this issue will remain crucial for the strategic challenge of preparedness. Thus while the predictive sciences are certainly relevant to the performance of practically wise action, they cannot fully describe it, and in turn, they can never replace it. In that light, a greater understanding of practical wisdom in organizations can only be developed using research methods that focus on description of, and deliberation about the unique, historical, contextual circumstances for action rather than the generalizable conditions and universally valid hypotheses.

Thus even if our research questions address the aesthetic dimensions of practice, we may still mistakenly identify the importance of practical wisdom for strategic preparedness if we do not use appropriate research methods to address them. In this regard, we suggest that the methodological pluralism expressed on the strategy-as-practice website, as well as the critical and philosophical perspectives adopted within the organizational aesthetics discourses, can be supported and extended by the notion of 'phronetic social science'.

Some organizational scholars have already explicitly considered the question of method with regard to practical wisdom. Broadly, it would appear that not only is the concept of practical wisdom relevant for organizational practice, but additionally it may provide a new epistemological basis for the embodied, intentional practice of

---

[97] For an analysis of this concept and its relevance to strategic management, cf. Prahalad and Bettis (1986); Bettis and Prahalad (1995); and Von Krogh and Roos (1996).

organizational research. Bent Flyvbjerg has taken the most dramatic steps in this direction, writing that:

> Phronetic social science explores historic circumstances and current practices to find avenues to praxis. The task of phronetic social science is to clarify and deliberate about the problems and risks we face and to outline how things may be done differently, in full knowledge that we cannot find ultimate answers to these questions or even a single version of what the questions are. (2001: 140)

Olaf Eikeland picks up on this line of argument and connects it at an epistemological level with the existing tradition of collaborative action inquiry in the social sciences:

> My interpretation of Aristotle's orientation toward practice does not, however, focus unilaterally on prudence as an alternative to, or even a replacement for, theoretical reason, but rather, as indicated, on a different interpretation of theoretical reason itself. (Eikeland, 2001: 148)

In an attempt to describe the implications of the Aristotelian concept of practical wisdom as a description of those forms of embodied, intentional action that are qualitatively or normatively valuable or better, Roland Calori writes:

> Following a pragmatic epistemology, the researcher and the researched should share time-space and action-reflection in face-to-face situations, in order to generate knowledge of acquaintance and transform it into knowledge about. (Calori, 2002: 878)

Finally, after a personal reflection on his own struggle to remain anonymous and objective in his research practices

Roos (2005) concluded that phronetic research may be both more interesting for scholars and practitioners alike simply

> because this field is about humans interacting. Escaping into the convention of third-person anonymity may be counterproductive.

We suggest that the methods appropriate for research focused on practical wisdom involve direct contact with, and engagement in, organizational practice, as well as a corresponding, pragmatic intention to describe that practice in ways that inform deliberations about whether that practice is normatively optimal.

As a provisional example of phronetic social science, our endeavor in this book is to bring different streams of organizational and strategic management research into contact with each other by raising new questions and identifying points for future research and dialogue. Concretely, we have presented the dynamic model of practical wisdom as a framework with which to describe and deliberate about specific practices in organizations where people struggle to become more prepared for unexpected change. In this respect, we hope both to generate greater understanding of practical wisdom in organizations, and at the same time, to contribute to the development of wise practices that enable organizations to become more strategically prepared.

18.0
Recommendations for the Field of Preparedness

In closing, we frame this book as an example of phronetic social science (Flyvbjerg, 2001) that seeks both to describe and to deliberate about a practical phenomenon. Having therefore described what we see as the importance of practical wisdom for strategic preparedness in organizations, we frame our deliberations as recommendations offered directly to various practitioners – on the front lines of the 'war on terror', in the executive offices of multinational firms, at business schools, and in the everyday circumstances of organizational life – who are currently struggling to become more strategically prepared for unexpected change.

18.1 The front lines

To the people on the front lines of the 'war on terror', we offer recognition for the personal sacrifices in support of preparedness objectives that have been made following the events of 9/11. In reference to the strategic model of preparedness that we introduced above, we believe that many of these efforts have extended the limits of the thinkable, and that the existing resource capacity has in some cases been optimized in the face of the limits of the possible. The renewed international dialogue, the increased inter-agency collaboration within national governments, the improvement of emergency response capacity, and so on: such activities have without a doubt increased levels of preparedness in response to similarly catastrophic events.

At the same time, we believe that some of these same efforts have not effectively mitigated the threats, but resulted in blowback instead (for example, Abu Ghraib), while other well-intended efforts have resulted in squander (for example, highest per capita Homeland Security expenditures in Utah). All in all, in view of protracted military engagement, failure to mitigate the impacts of natural catastropoles, the unresolved economic and social challenges associated with globalization, we continue to question whether the 'failure of imagination' and the 'failure of leadership' have yet been adequately addressed by the international community.[98]

In view of these practical problems, our simple message to the people at the front lines is: don't underestimate the importance of *ethics*. Every time anyone defines a risk as 'acceptable' or not, a value judgment is being made. Even the development of scenarios that mark or stretch the limits of the thinkable (for example, 'a million casualties') involves ethical considerations. In this light, ethics appears not as a secondary afterthought, but rather as a primary concern of direct relevance to any strategic response to the need for preparedness. We therefore call for more direct orientation toward ethics among those people who serve 'on the front lines' of the preparedness field.

18.2 Business leaders and strategists

With regard to the leaders who are seeking to make their organizations more strategically prepared not only for

---

[98] We refer here to two of the failures identified in the 9/11 Commission Report.

terrorist threats, but also for the uncertainty that is endemic to today's global business environment, we recognize the efforts that they are taking to minimize risk and ensure the continuity (no less than the sustainable growth) of their operations. Increased data security, more advanced risk modeling and assessment procedures, improved security measures designed to protect both employees and fixed assets: such activities have undoubtedly made organizations more prepared to respond to unexpected, and potentially disastrous events.

At the same time, we suggest that the levels of investment in systems and infrastructure improvements have not been matched by similar investments in people. Specifically, in our research we have seen relatively few deliberate attempts to cultivate the habits of mind and body required to utilize those investments wisely, and even fewer (if any) attempts to cultivate practical wisdom through a general management educational program. Instead, we see continued cults of personality driven by hubris at the top and hero-worship in the ranks – and as CEO after CEO is led to jail in handcuffs, we wonder, how can everyone continue to pretend to be surprised?

In view of these practical problems, our message to organizational leaders is: don't underestimate the importance of *people* for preparedness. We acknowledge and support the development and implementation of preparedness standards for private- and public-sector organizations.[99] However, because people in organizations will undoubtedly find themselves justifying certain decisions

---

[99] We have learned about these efforts primarily through Bill Raisch, Director of the International Center for Enterprise Preparedness (InterCEP), a program housed within the Center for Catastrophe Preparedness and Response (CCPR) at New York University (NYU). As noted previously, Matt Statler joined InterCEP after this manuscript had been completed.

and actions based not only on explicitly-formulated standards, codes of behavior and guidelines, but additionally on implicitly-held values, they need practically wise habits in addition to expert knowledge and cutting-edge resources. Indeed, the balance of time horizons, interests, and responses to the environment cannot be implemented exclusively in accordance with a standard – instead, experientially-based practical wisdom must guide the development as well as the implementation of preparedness-related standards and policies in organizations.

In this sense, our considerations here serve as a call for a genuine orientation toward those organizational practices that develop *people* who are prepared to deal strategically with unexpected change.

18.3   Management education and training

To the educators seeking to develop business leaders more capable of handling uncertainty, we recognize your efforts to transform the business school curriculum to make it more appropriate and relevant to today's world. Concerning the increased emphasis on action learning, simulations, internships, mentoring, and so on, we believe that innovations such as these can effectively prepare managers to be more prepared for unexpected surprises at work.

At the same time, business schools continue to cling to their heritage, and the pedagogical methods, instructional materials, and physical setting remain rooted primarily the tradition of 'scientific management'. Most management education continues to focus on the transmission of scientifically-grounded concepts, models, and techniques, and on the inculcation of generic analytic skills.

In view of these practical limitations, our message to educators is: don't forget about the *normative* and *embodied* aspects of human experience. We believe that historical contexts, embodied perceptions, and subjective considerations are just as important for effective management as the rational, objective, and observer-independent 'laws' and 'principles' of markets and governance. Our considerations therefore additionally serve as a call for more active orientation toward hands-on, playful, and aesthetic learning processes in business schools and management development programs.[100]

18.4 Organizing in a complex and uncertain world

And finally, to all the people in today's complex and uncertain world who struggle to organize as they face the strategic challenge of preparedness, our message is simple: don't look past the *everyday* aspect of strategic preparedness.

Because the human social world cannot be fully controlled or predicted, the need for preparedness arises every day, to a greater or lesser degree of intensity. In our research, we have engaged with people who are serving on the front lines, working as organizational leaders, and educating the current and next generations of managers. While the intensity of the perceived need for preparedness varies widely among these different groups of people, they all feel it as they face the unexpected in their everyday lives.

Having undertaken this inquiry into the field, our main finding is that opportunities to cultivate the practical wisdom needed for strategic preparedness also arise everyday: from a 'user error' message on your computer screen to the simulation of chemical attack – from a surprise voice mail from a colleague to an all-day offsite

---

[100] At about the time this book was published Johan Roos became the Dean of MBA Programs at the Stockholm School of Economics (SSE). We shall see what happens with these programs.

planning retreat – from a structured project to a happy hour conversation with someone who works down the hall – from an asynchronous virtual training session to a two-year degree program.

All of these events stretch the limits of the thinkable and the possible to a greater or lesser degree. All of them call for practices that strike balances between different interests, time horizons, and orientations toward the environment. All of them are mediated by more or less dynamic changes in mode, medium, and milieu. And all of them provide an occasion to enact the common good by responding ethically and effectively.

In this sense, as any of us respond with practical wisdom to unexpected change, we develop everyday strategic preparedness for ourselves, for our organizations and for our communities.

References

Abizadeh, A. (2002) 'The Passions of the Wise: Phronesis, Rhetoric and Aristotle's Passionate Political Deliberation', *The Review of Metaphysics*, 56: 267–296.

Abrahamson, Eric (2004) *Change without Pain: How Managers Can Overcome Initiative Overload, Organizational Chaos and Employee Burnout,* Harvard Business School Press.

Addleson, Mark (1996) 'Resolving the Spirit and Substance of Organizational Learning', *Journal of Organizational Change Management*, 9 (1): 32–41.

Aldrich, H.E. (1979) *Organizations and Environments.* Englewood Cliffs, NJ: Prentice-Hall.

Anderson, Benedict (1991) *Imagined Communities: Reflections on the Origin and Spread of Nationalism,* Revised ed. New York: Verso.

Anscombe, G.E.M. (1963) *Intention* (2nd ed.). Oxford: Blackwell.

Ansoff, H.I. (1965) *Corporate Strategy: An Analytic Approach to Business Policy for Growth and Expansion.* New York: McGraw-Hill.

Ardelt, M. (2004) 'Wisdom as Expert Knowledge System: A Critical Review of a Contemporary Operationalization of an Ancient Concept?' *Human Development,* (47): 257–85.

Argyris, Chris (1992) *On Organizational Learning.* Cambridge, Massachusetts: Blackwell.

Argyris, C., D. Schon and M. Payne (eds) (1995) *Organizational Learning II: Theory, Method, and Practice.* 2nd Edition. Addison-Wesley Pub Co.

Aristotle (1962) *Nicomachean Ethics.* Indianapolis: Bobbs-Merrill.

Badiou, Alain (2001) *Ethics: A Chapter on the Understanding of Evil.* New York: Verso.

Bakhtin, Mikhail (1990) *Art and Answerability: Early Philosophical Chapters.* Austin: University of Texas Press.

Balfour, Danny L. and Mesaros, William (1994) 'Connecting the Local Narratives: Public Administration as a Hermeneutic Science', *Public Administration Review,* 54 (6): 559–64.

Balogun, J., A. Sigismund Huff and P. Johnson (2003) 'Three Responses to the Methodological Challenges of Studying Strategizing', *Journal of Management Studies*, 40 (1): 198–224.

Baltes, P. and U. Kunzmann (2004) 'The Two Faces of Wisdom: Wisdom as a General Theory of Knowledge and Judgment about Excellence in Mind and Virtue vs Wisdom as Everyday Realisation in People and Products. *Human Development*, 47: 290–299.

Barrett, F.J. (1998) 'Creativity and Improvisation in Jazz and Organizations: Implications for Organizational Learning', *Organization Science*, 9 (5): 605–22.

Bateson, G. (1987) *Steps to an Ecology of Mind: Collected Chapters in Anthropology, Psychiatry, Evolution, and Epistemology*. Northvale, N.J.: Aronson.

Baumard, Phillippe (1999) *Tacit Knowledge in Organizations*. Thousand Oaks, California: Sage.

Baumhart, R.C. (1961) 'How Ethical Are Businessmen?', *Harvard Business Review* (July–August): 6–17.

Beck, U. (1992) *Risk Society*. London: Sage.

Berge, T. (1990) *The First 24 Hours*, Cambridge MA: Basil Blackwell.

Bettelheim, B. (1943) 'Individual and Mass Behavior in Extreme Situations', *Journal of Abnormal and Social Psychology*, 38: 417–52.

Bettis, R., and C.K. Prahalad (1995) 'The Dominant Logic: Retrospective and Extension', *Strategic Management Journal*, 16 (1): 5–14.

Beunza, D. and D. Stark (2003) 'The Organization of Responsiveness: Innovation and Recovery in the Trading Rooms of Lower Manhattan', *Socio-Economic Review*, 1: 135–64.

Blaug, R. (2000) 'Citizenship and Political Judgment: Between Discourse Ethics and Phronesis', *Res Publica*, 6: 179–98.

Botan, C. (1997) 'Ethics in Strategic Communication Campaigns: The Case for a New Approach to Public Relations', *The Journal of Business Communication*, 34: 188–202.

Bourdieu, P. (1990) *The Logic of Practice*. Stanford University Press.

Bourdieu, P. (1998) *Practical Reason*. Stanford University Press.

Brenner, S.N., and E.A. Molander (1977) 'Is the Ethics of Business Changing?', *Harvard Business Review* (January–February): 57–71.

Buber, Martin (1970) *I and Thou.* New York: Scribner.
Burgoyne, J.G. (1994) 'Stakeholder Analysis', in C. Cassell and G. Symon (eds) *Qualititative Methods in Organizational Research: A Practical Guide*, pp. 187–207. New Delhi: Sage.
Butler, Judith (1999) *Gender Trouble: Feminism and the Subversion of Identity.* New York: Routledge.
Caillois, Roger (1961) *Man, Play and Games.* Chicago: University of Illinois Press.
Calori, R. (2002) 'Real Time/Real Space Research: Connecting Action and Reflection in Organizational Studies', *Organization Studies*, 23 (6): 877–83.
Certeau, Michel de (1984) *The Practice of Everyday Life.* Berkeley: University of California Press.
Chakravarthy, B., and Y. Doz (1992) 'Strategy Process Research: Focusing on Corporate Self-Renewal', *Strategic Management Journal*, 13: 5–14.
Clegg, S., M. Kornberger and C. Rhodes (2005) 'Learning/Becoming/Organizing'. *Organization*, 12 (2): 147–67.
Clegg, S., and A. Ross-Smith (2003) 'Revisiting the Boundaries: Management Education and Learning in a Post-positivist World', *Academy of Management Learning & Education*, 2 (1): 85–98.
Cohen, W.M., and D.A. Leventhal (1990) 'Absorptive Capacity: A New Perspective on Learning and Innovation', *Administrative Science Quarterly*, 35: 128–52.
Council on Foreign Relations Independent Task Force (2003) *Emergency Responders: Drastically Underfunded, Dangerously Unprepared*, www.cfr.org.
Crossan, Mary (1998) 'Improvisation in Action', *Organization Science*, (9) 5: 593–99.
Csikszentmihalyi, Mihaly (1990) *Flow: The Psychology of Optimal Experience.* New York: Harper & Row.
Cummings, S., and D. Wilson (2003) *Images of Strategy.* Oxford: Blackwell.
Czarniawska, Barbara (1997) *Narrating the Organization: Dramas of Institutional Identity.* University of Chicago Press.
Davidson, James (1997) *Courtesan and Fishcakes: The Consuming Passions of Classical Athens.* New York: St. Martins Press.
De Bono, Edward (1992) *Serious Creativity: Using the Power of Lateral Thinking to Create New Ideas.* New York: HarperBusiness.

De Wit, B., and R. Meyer (2001) *Strategy. Process, Content, Context* (2nd ed.). London: Thomson Learning.

Deleuze, Gilles (1994) *Difference and Repetition*. New York: Columbia University Press.

Deloitte Research (2003) *The Homeland Security Market: The World's Most Challenging Business Environment*, A Deloitte Research Public Sector Study, http://www.dc.com/Insights/research/public/homeland_security.asp.

Denning, Stephen (2000) *The Springboard: How Storytelling Ignites Action in Knowledge-Era Organizations*. Boston: Butterworth-Heinemann.

Detienne, M. and J.P. Vernant (1974) *Cunning Intelligence in Greek Culture & Society*. University of Chicago Press.

Dreyfus, H., and S. Dreyfus (1986) *Mind Over Machine: The Power of Human Intuition and Expertise: The Era of the Computer*. New York: Free Press.

Eikeland, O. (2001) 'Action Research as the Hidden Curriculum of the Western Tradition', in *Handbook of Action Research: Participative Inquiry and Practice*, ed. P. Reason and H. Bradbury. London: Sage.

Eisenhardt, K. (1989) 'Building Theories from Case Study Research', *Academy of Management Review*, 14 (4): 532–50.

Erikson, Erik (1964) *Childhood and Society*. New York: Norton.

Farjoun, M. (2002) 'Towards an Organic Perspective on Strategy', *Strategic Management Journal*, 23 (7): 561–94.

Fink, S. (1986) *Crisis Management: Planning for the Inevitable*, New York: America Management Association.

Flyvbjerg, B. (2001) *Making Social Science Matter: Why Social Inquiry Fails and How It Can Succeed Again*. Cambridge University Press.

Fontrodona, J., and D. Melé (2002) 'Philosophy as a Base for Management: An Aristotelian Integrative Proposal Reason in Practice', *The Journal of Philosophy of Management* (2) 2.

Foucault, M. (1980) *Power/Knowledge: Selected Interviews and Other Writings, 1972–1977*. Brighton, Sussex: Harvester Press.

Freydberg, B. (1997) *The Play of the Platonic Dialogues*. New York: Peter Lang.

Gadamer, H.G. (2002 [1960]) *Truth and Method*. New York: Continuum.

Gallagher, S. (1993) 'The Place of Phronesis in Postmodern Hermeneutics', *Philosophy Today*, 37: 298–305.

Gallagher, S., and F. Varela (2001), 'Redrawing the Map and Resetting the Time: Phenomenology and the Cognitive Sciences.' In *The Reach of Reflection: The Future of Phenomenology*, ed. Steven Crowell, Lester Embree and Samuel J. Julian. Electronpress. Electronic publication.

Geus, Arie de (1997) *The Living Company*. Boston: Harvard Business School Press.

Goshal, S. (2005) 'Bad Management Theories Are Destroying Good Management Practice', *Academy of Management Learning and Education*, 4 (1): 75–91.

Guillet de Monthoux, P. (2004) *The Art Firm: Aesthetic Management and Metaphysical Marketing*. Palo Alto: Stanford University Press.

Guth, W.D. (1985) *Handbook of Business Strategy*. Boston MA: Warren, Gorham & Lamont.

Habermas, J. (1987) *The Philosophical Discourse of Modernity: Twelve Lectures*. Cambridge, Mass.: MIT Press.

Halverson, R. (2004) 'Accessing, Documenting and Communicating Practical Wisdom: The Phronesis of School Leadership Practice'. *American Journal of Education*, III: 90–121.

Hamel, G. (1996) 'Strategy as Revolution', *Harvard Business Review*, 74 (4) (July–August): 69–73.

Hamel, G., and C.K. Prahalad (1989) 'Strategic Intent', *Harvard Business Review* (May–June): 63–76.

Harris, C. (1999) *Art and Innovation: The Xerox PARC Artist-in-Residence Program*. Cambridge: MIT Press.

Hatch, M.J. (1999) 'Exploring the Empty Spaces of Organizing: How Improvisational Jazz Helps Redescribe Organizational Structure', *Organization Studies*, 20 (1): 75–100.

Hatch, M.J. (1996) 'The Role of the Researcher: An Analysis of Narrative Position in Organization Theory', *Journal of Management Inquiry*, 5 (4): 359–374.

Heidegger, M. (1962) *Being and Time*. Trans. John Macquarrie and Edward Robinson. Oxford: Blackwell.

Heidegger, M. (1982) *Basic Problems of Phenomenology*. Trans. A. Hofstadter. Indianapolis: Indiana University Press.

Hendry, D.F. (2000) 'On Detectable and Non-detectable Structural Change'. *Structural Change and Economic Dynamics*, 11: 45–65.

Hendry, J., and D. Seidl (2003) 'The Structure and Significance of Strategic Episodes: Social Systems Theory and the Routine Practices of Strategic Change', *Journal of Management Studies*, 40 (1): 175–96.

Heracleous, L. (2003) *Strategy and Organization: Realizing Strategic Management*. Cambridge University Press.

Heracleous, L., and M. Barrett (2001) 'Organizational Change as Discourse: Communicative Actions and Deep Structures in the Context of IT Implementation', *Academy of Management Journal*, 44 (4): 755–78.

Hersh, S. (2004) *Chain of Command: The Road from 9/11 to Abu Ghraib*. Harper Collins.

Hodgkinson, G.P. (2005) *Images of Competitive Space: A Study – Managerial and Organizational Strategic Cognition*. Basingstoke: Palgrave Macmillan.

Hodgkinson, G.P., and G. Wright (2002) 'Confronting Strategic Inertia in a Top Management Team: Learning from Failure.' *Organization Studies*, 23 (6): 949–78.

Hofer, C., and D. Schendel (1978) *Strategy Formulation: Analytical Concepts*. St. Paul: West Publishing Company.

Hoffman, B. (2002) 'Medicine as Practical Wisdom (Phronesis)', *Poesis Prax*, 1: 135–149.

Hoskisson, R.E. et al. (1999) 'Swings of a Pendulum', *Journal of Management* (25): 417–56.

Huizinga, Johan (1950) *Homo Ludens: A Study of the Play Element in Culture*. Boston: Beacon Press.

Irigaray, Luce (1985) *Speculum of the Other Woman*. Ithaca, N.Y.: Cornell University Press.

Jacobs, C., and M. Statler (2005) 'Strategy Creation as Serious Play'. In S.W. Floyd, J. Roos, C. Jacobs and F. Kellermans (eds), *Innovating Strategy Process*. Oxford: Blackwell.

Jacobs, C. and Statler, M. (2006) 'Toward a Technology of Foolishness – Developing Scenarios through Serious Play' *International Studies of Management and Organisation*, 36(3): 77–92.

Jaksa, J. A. and Pritchard, M. S. (1994) *Communications Ethics: Methods of Analysis*. Belmont, Calif.: Wadsworth Publishing Company.

Jarzabkowski, P. (2004) 'Strategy as Practice: Recursiveness, Adaptation and Practices in Use'. *Organization Studies*, 25 (4): 529–60.

Johnson, G. (2004) *Exploring Corporate Strategy. Text and Cases*, 7th ed., London: FT Prentice Hall.

Johnson, G., L. Melin and R. Whittington (2003) 'Guest Editor's Introduction: Micro Strategy and Strategizing: Towards an Activity-based View', *Journal of Management Studies*, 40 (1): 3–22.

Kirkeby, O. (2003) 'The Greek Square, or, The Normative Challenge of Aesthetics', *Ephemera*, Critical dialogues on organisations.

Kohlberg, L. (1981) *Philosophy of Moral Development*. New York: Harper & Row Publishers.

Kriwet, C. (1997) *Inter- and Intraorganizational Knowledge Transfer*, Doctoral Dissertation, Universität St. Gallen, Nr. 2063.

Kronman, A. (1995) *The Lost Lawyer*, Cambridge: Harvard University Press.

Levinas, E. (1989) *The Levinas Reader*, ed. Sean Hand. Oxford: Blackwell.

Linstead, S., and H. Hopfl (2000) *The Aesthetics of Organization*. Thousand Oaks, Calif.: Sage.

Lynch, R. (1999) 'Seeking Practical Wisdom', *Business and Economic History*, 28 (2): 123–135.

MacIntyre, A. (1981) *After Virtue: A Study in Moral Theory*. University of Notre Dame Press.

Maguire, S. (1997) 'Business Ethics: A Compromise between Politics and Virtue', *Journal of Business Ethics*, 16: 1411–18.

McKinley, W., and M. Mone (2002) 'Foresight As Enactment: Organizations As Producers Of Environments', conference paper presented at *Probing the Future: Developing Organizational Foresight in the Knowledge Economy*, University of Strathclyde, July 11–13.

Merleau-Ponty, M. (1962) *The Phenomenology of Perception*. London: Routledge.

Mintzberg, H. (1994) *The Rise and Fall of Strategic Planning: Reconceiving Roles for Planning, Plans, Planners*. New York: Prentice Hall.

Mintzberg, H. (2004) *Managers Not MBA's: A Hard Look at the Soft Practice of Managing and Management Development.* San Francisco: Berrett-Koehler Publishers.

Mintzberg, H., and J.A. Waters (1985) 'Of Strategies, Deliberate and Emergent', *Strategic Management Review,* 6 (July): 257–72.

Mintzberg, H., B. Ahlstrand and J. Lampel (1998a) *Strategy Safari.* Englewood Cliffs, NJ: Prentice Hall.

Mintzberg, H., J.B. Quinn and S. Ghoshal (1998b) *The Strategy Process.* New York: Prentice Hall.

Mitroff, I., P. Srivastava and F. Udwadia (1987) 'Effective Crisis Management', *Academy of Management Executive,* 1: 282–92.

Mitroff, I. and D. Swanson (2004) 'An Open Letter to the Deans and Faculties of American Business Schools: A Call for Action. *The Academy of Management News,* 35: 7–8.

Mitroff, I. (1984) *Corporate Tragedies, Product Tempering, Sabotage, and Other Catastrophes,* with Ralph Kilmann. New York: Praeger.

Mitroff, I. (1986) 'Teaching Corporate America to Think About Crisis Prevention,' *Journal of Business Strategy,* 6 (4): 40–47.

Mitroff, I., and M. Alpaslan, (2003) 'Preparing for Evil', *Harvard Business Review* (April): 109–15.

Moingeon, B., and A.C. Edmondson (1996) *Organizational Learning and Competitive Advantage.* Thousand Oaks, CA: Sage Publications.

Montgomery, C.A., and M.E. Porter (1991) *Strategy: Seeking and Securing Competitive Advantage.* Boston: Harvard Business School Press.

Moorman, C., and A.S. Miner (1998a) 'The Convergence of Planning and Execution: Improvisation in New Product Development', *Journal of Marketing,* (62) 3: 1–20.

Moorman, C., and A.S. Miner (1998b) 'Organizational Improvisation and Organizational Memory', *Academy of Management Review,* (23) 4: 698–723.

Mugerauer, R. (1996) *Interpreting Environments: Traditions, Deconstruction, Hermeneutics.* Austin: University of Texas Press.

Noel, J. (1999a) 'Phronesis and Phantasia: Teaching with Wisdom and Imagination', *Journal of Philosophy of Education,* 33 (2): 277–87.

Noel, J. (1999b) 'On the Varieties of Phronesis', *Educational Philosophy and Theory,* 31 (3).

Nonaka, I., and H. Takeuchi, (1995) *The Knowledge-Creating Company: How Japanese Companies Create the Dynamics of Innovation.* New York: Oxford University Press.

Nussbaum, M. (2001) *The Fragility of Goodness: Luck and Ethics: Greek Tragedy and Philosophy.* Updated edition. Cambridge University Press.

Nystrom, P.C., and Starbuck, W.H. (1984) 'To Avoid Organizational Crises, Unlearn', *Organizational Dynamics,* 12: 53–65.

Oliver, D., and J. Roos (2000) *Striking a Balance: Complexity and Knowledge Landscapes.* Maidenhead: McGraw-Hill.

Oliver, D., and J. Roos (2005) 'Decision-making in High Velocity Environments: The Importance of Guiding Principles', *Organization Studies* 26 (6): 889–913.

Orlikowski, W. (2000) 'Using Technology and Constituting Structures: A Practice Lens for Studying Technology – Organizations'. *Organization Science,* 11 (4): 404–28.

Piaget, J. (1958) *Etudes d'épistémologie génétique,* vol. V. Paris: Presses Universitaires de France.

Polanyi, M. (1976) 'Tacit Knowledge'. In M. Marx and F. Goodson (eds), *Theories – Contemporary Psychology.* New York: Macmillan, 330–44.

Porter, M. (1980) *Competitive Strategy: Techniques for Analyzing Industries and Competitors.* New York: Free Press.

PriceWaterhouseCoopers. (2004) *Managing Risk: An Assessment of CEO Preparedness.* Http://www.pwc.com.

Purser, R., C. Park, and A. Montuori, (1995) 'Limits to Anthropocentrism: Toward an Ecocentric Organization Paradigm?' *Academy of Management Review,* 20 (4): 1053–89.

Regner, P. (2003) 'Strategy Creation in the Periphery: Inductive Versus Deductive Strategy Making', *Journal of Management Studies,* 40 (1): 58–82.

Ricoeur, P. (1986) *Du texte à l'action,* Paris: Editions de Seuil.

Ricoeur, P. (1991). *From Text to Action.* Evanston, Ill.: Northwestern University Press.

Roos, J. (2005) 'I Matter: Remaining the First Author in Strategy Research,' in S. Floyd, J. Roos, F. Kellerman and C. Jacobs (eds), *Innovating Strategy Processes.* Blackwell: Oxford, 252–62.

Roos, J. (2006) *Thinking from Within: A Hands-on Strategy Practice*. Basingstoke: Palgrave Macmillan.

Roos, G., and J. Roos (1997) 'Measuring Your Company's Intellectual Performance'. *Long Range Planning*, 30 (3): 413–26.

Roos, J., G. Roos, N.C. Dragonetti and L. Edvinsson (1997) *Intellectual Capital: Navigating the New Business Landscape*. London: Macmillan.

Roos, J., and M. Roos (2006) 'On Spontaneity', Working paper 72, Imagination Lab Foundation, Switzerland www. imagilab.org).

Roos, J., and B. Victor (1999) 'Towards a Model of Strategy Making as Serious Play', *European Management Journal*, 17 (4): 348–55.

Roos, J., B. Victor and M. Statler (2004) 'Playing Seriously with Strategy', *Long Range Planning*, 37 (6) (December): 549–68.

Rorty, R. (1979) *Philosophy and the Mirror of Nature*. Princeton: Princeton University Press.

Sandelands, L., and G.C. Buckner (1989) 'Of Art and Work: Aesthetic Experience and the Psychology of Work Feelings', in L.L. Cummings and B.M. Staw (eds), *Research in Organizational Behavior*. Greenwich, CT: JAI Press.

Scharmer, C. (2001) 'Self-Transcending Knowledge: Sensing and Organizing around Emerging Opportunities', *Journal of Knowledge Management*, 5 (2): 137–50.

Schein, E. (1993) 'On Dialogue, Culture and Organizational Learning', *Organizational Dynamics*, 22 (2): 40–51.

Schoemaker, P.J. (1993) 'Multiple Scenario Development: Its Conceptual and Behavioral Foundation', *Strategic Management Journal*, 14 (3): 193.

Schoemaker, P.J. (1995) 'Scenario Planning: A Tool for Strategic Thinking.' *Sloan Management Review*, 36 (2): 25.

Schwartz, P. (1991) *The Art of the Long View*. New York: Doubleday/Currency.

Schweinsberg, M., J.-H. Andne, J. Roos and G. von Krogle (1997) 'The Berlingske Group: Looking at the Future of Electronic Media', IMD Case Study, GM 656.

Searle, J. (1983) *Intentionality. A Chapter in the Philosophy of Mind*. Cambridge University Press.

Selener, D. (1997) *Participatory Action Research and Social Change*. Ithaca, NY: The Cornell Participatory Action Research Network, Cornell University.

Silva Marques, C. (2002) 'Anthony Kronman on the Virtue of Practical Wisdom', *Ratio Juris*, 15 (3): 328–40.

Smith, T. (1999) 'Aristotle on the Conditions for and Limits of the Common Good', *American Political Science Review*, 93 (3): 625–37.

Stacey, R. (1996) *Complexity and Creativity in Organizations*. San Francisco: Berrett-Koehler Publishers.

Starik, M., and G. Rands (1995) 'Weaving an Integrated Web: Multilevel and Multisystem Perspectives of Ecologically Sustainable Organizations', *Academy of Management Review*, 20 (4): 908–35.

Statler, M. (2005) 'Practical Wisdom and Serious Play: Reflections on Management Understanding'. In H. Schrat (ed.), *Sophisticated Survival Techniques/Strategies in Art and Economy*. Berlin: Kulturverlag Kadmos.

Statler, M., and P. Guillet de Monthoux (forthcoming) 'Aesthetic Play as an Organizing Principle'. In D. Barry and H. Hansen (eds), *New and Emerging Approaches to Management and Organization*. London: Sage.

Statler, M., and J. Roos (2006) 'Re-framing Strategic Preparedness: An Essay on Practical Wisdom'. *International Journal of Management Concept and Philosophy*, 2 (2): 99–117.

Statler, M., J. Roos and B. Victor (2006) 'Illustrating the Need for Practical Wisdom'. *International Journal of Management Concepts and Philosophy*, 2 (1): 1–30.

Stern, R. (1997) 'The Rule of Wisdom and the Rule of Law in Plato's Statesman', *American Political Science Review*, 91 (2): 264–76.

Sternberg, R. (1998) 'A Balance Theory of Wisdom', *Review of General Psychology*, 2 (4): 347–65.

Sternberg, R. (2001) 'Why Schools Should Teach for Wisdom: the Balance Theory of Wisdom in Education', *Educational Psychologist*, 36 (4): 227–45.

Sternberg, R. (2004) 'Words to the Wise about Wisdom'. *Human Development*, (47): 286–9.

Strati, A. (1999) *Organization and Aesthetics*. Thousand Oaks: Sage.

Sutton-Smith, B. (1997) *The Ambiguity of Play*. Cambridge, Mass.: Harvard University Press.

Taylor, C. (1993) 'Explanation and Practical Reason'. In M. Nussbaum and A. Sen (eds), *The Quality of Life*. Oxford: Clarendon, 208–31.

Taylor, S.S., and H. Hanson (2005) 'Finding Form: Looking at the Field of Organizational Aesthetics.' *Journal of Management Studies*, 42 (6): 1211–32.

Thiele, Leslie Paul (2000) 'Common Sense, Judgment and the Limits of Political Theory', *Political Theory*, 28: 565–88.

Thomas, H., and T. Hafsi (2005) 'The Field of Strategy: In Search of a Walking Stick', *European Management Journal*, 23 (5): 507–19.

Thompson, J.D. (1956) 'On Building an Administrative Science'. *Administrative Science Quarterly*, 1: 102–11.

Trevino, L. (1985) 'Ethical Decision Making in Organizations: A Person-Situation Interactionist Model', *Academy of Management Review*, 11 (3): 601–17.

Tsoukas, H., and R. Chia (2002) 'On Organizational Becoming: Rethinking Organizational Change'. *Organization Science*, 13 (5) (September–October): 567–82.

Tsoukas, H., and S. Cummings (1997) 'Marginalization and Recovery: The Emergence of Aristotelian Themes in Organization Studies', *Organization Studies*, 18 (4): 655–83.

Tyson, L., and N. Andrews (2004) 'The Upwardly Global MBA', *Strategy+Business* (Autumn): 67.

Van de Ven, A.H. (1992) 'Suggestions for Studying Strategy Process: A Research Note', *Strategic Management Journal*, 13: 169–88.

Van der Heijden, K. (1996) *Scenarios: The Art of Strategic Conversation*. New York: John Wiley & Sons.

Van der Heijden, K., R. Bradfield, G. Burt, G. Caiths and G. Wright (2002) *The Sixth Sense: Accelerating Organizational Learning with Scenarios*. New York: John Wiley.

Van Mannen, J. (1983) *Varieties of Qualitative Research*. Newbury Park: Sage.

Varela, F., E. Thompson and E. Rosch (1992) *The Embodied Mind*. Cambridge, MA: MIT Press.

Von Krogh, G., and J. Roos (1996) 'A Tale of the Unfinished', *Strategic Management Journal*, 17 (9): 729–37.

Von Wright, G.H. (1971) *Explanation and Understanding*. London: Routledge & Kegan Paul.

Vygotsky, L.S. (1978) *Mind in Society: The Development of Higher Psychological Processes*. Cambridge MA: Harvard University Press.

Weaver, G., L. Trevino, and P. Cochran (1999) 'Corporate Ethics Practices in the mid-1990's: An Empirical Study of the Fortune 1000', *Journal of Business Ethics*, 18 (3): 283–94.

Weick, K.E. (1988) 'Enacted Sensemaking in Crisis Situations', *Journal of Management Studies*, 25: 112–27.

Weick, K.E. (1993). 'The Collapse of Sensemaking in Organizations: The Mann Gluch Disaster', *Administrative Science Quarterly*, 38: 638–52.

Weick, K.E. (1995a) 'Organizational Redesign as Improvisation', in G.P. Huber and W.H. Glick (eds), *Organizational Change and Redesign*, 346–79. New York: Oxford University Press.

Weick, K.E. (1995b) *Sensemaking in Organizations*. Thousand Oaks: Sage.

Weick, K.E., and K. Sutcliffe (2001) *Managing the Unexpected: Assuring High Performance in an Age of Complexity*. San Francisco: Jossey-Bass.

Whetten D., G. Rands, and P. Godfrey (2001) 'What Are the Responsibilities of Business to Society?', in A. Pettigrew, H. Thomas and R. Whittington (eds) *Handbook of Strategy and Management*, London: Sage.

Whittington, R. (eds) (1993) *What Is Strategy and Does It Matter?* London: Routledge.

Whittington, R. (2002) 'The Work of Strategizing and Organizing: For a Practice Perspective', *Strategic Organization*, 1 (1): 119–27.

Wilson, D., and P. Jarzabkowski (2004) 'Thinking and Acting Strategically: New Challenges for Interrogating Strategy'. *European Management Journal*, 1: 14–20.

Yin, R. (1981) 'The Case Study Crisis: Some Answers', *Administrative Science Quarterly*, 26: 58–65.

Yin, R. (1994) *Case Study Research: Design and Methods*, 2nd edition, Thousand Oaks: Sage.

Index